Guide to
SEABIRDS
of Southern Africa

Peter Ryan

Dedication:
*To John Cooper, who taught me about
seabirds and so much more*

Published by Struik Nature
(an imprint of Penguin Random House
South Africa (Pty) Ltd)
Reg. No. 1953/000441/07

The Estuaries No. 4, Oxbow Crescent,
Century Avenue, Century City, 7441
PO Box 1144, Cape Town, 8000 South Africa

Visit **www.struiknature.co.za** and join the
Struik Nature Club for updates, news, events
and special offers.

First published in 2017
Second edition published in 2023

10 9 8 7 6 5 4 3 2 1

Print: 978 1 77584 847 9
ePUB: 978 1 77584 848 6

Publisher: Pippa Parker
Managing editor: Roelien Theron
Editors: Emsie du Plessis, Colette Alves
Designer: Gillian Black
Proofreader: Helen de Villiers

Reproduction by Resolution Colour (Pty) Ltd, Cape Town
  and Studio Repro
Printed and bound in China by 1010 Printing
  International Ltd

Front cover: Black-browed Albatross (Marc – Stock.
Adobe.com)
Back cover: (clockwise) Antarctic Tern; Cape Petrel;
Northern Rockhopper Penguin; Tawny Leopardwing
Spine: Cape Gannet (Peter Hayman – Penguin
Random House)
Title page: African Penguins (Chris Fallows)
Contents page: (top to bottom) Shy Albatross; Tahiti
Petrel (Kirk Zufelt); Red-footed Booby; Crozet Shag;
flying squid

ACKNOWLEDGEMENTS

This book wouldn't be possible without the
contributions of the photographers who supplied
images: Mike Buckham, Rohan Clarke, Daniel
Danckwerts, Ben Dilley, Cliff Dorse, Rich Everett, Chris
Fallows, Paul Gale, John Graham, Trevor Hardaker,
Chris Jones, Ferran López, Albert McLean, Dan Mantle,
Michael Mason, Matxalen Pauly Salinas Christian Perez,
Niall Perrins, Mike Pope, Adam Riley, Dom Rollinson,
Barrie Rose, Stefan Schoombie, Hadoram Shirihai,
Chris Sloan, Hiroyuki Tanoi, Gary Thoburn, Berry van
der Hoorn, Otto Whitehead, Michelle and Peter Wong,
Mark Yates, Steve Young and especially Kirk Zufelt,
who generously supplied many images for this edition.
Bob Flood kindly assisted with sourcing images, and
Susan Mill and Mathieu Rouault provided the maps.
Steve Howell helped name the flying fish images.

I am grateful to the many birders and seabird
biologists who have shared my seabird adventures
over the years: Graeme Avery and John Cooper
for the early beach patrols, John Graham for many
hours sea-watching from headlands, Harry Dilley
who helped me overcome my dislike of small-boat
pelagics, and especially Barrie Rose for introducing
me to the joys of birding at sea. I thank all the
people who have been on research cruises and
island trips over the past four decades.

From a scientific perspective, I have been
privileged to work with some great seabird
biologists, and to introduce many enthusiastic
students and field assistants to the joys of seabirds.
It is impossible to list them all, and unfair to
single out only a few. The South African Antarctic
research programme, in its various incarnations, has
supported my research over many years; thanks to
the team at the Department of Fisheries, Forestry
and the Environment, the crews of the many vessels
I have sailed on and the helicopter personnel
who have taken me to seabird islands. My deep
appreciation also goes to Pippa Parker and her team
at Struik Nature for their support.

This book is dedicated to John Cooper, who started
me on this adventure, helped train me as a scientist,
and initiated many of the long-term studies from
which my scientific career benefited. His gentle, caring
nature taught me much about being human. Finally,
heartfelt thanks to Coleen and Molly, for tolerating
my frequent absences, and for understanding my
need to spend time at sea and on seabird islands.

CONTENTS

Southern Africa supports a rich diversity of seabirds, including all families except the auks

INTRODUCTION

This book introduces the seabirds of southern Africa and the adjacent Southern Ocean. Much of the book is devoted to their identification, but it also describes their fascinating biology. Seabirds are birds that derive most of their food from the oceans. They include penguins, albatrosses, petrels and shearwaters, storm petrels, tropicbirds, frigatebirds, gannets and boobies, and alcids (auks, guillemots and puffins), as well as many species of cormorants, gulls and terns. Skuas and most phalaropes are largely terrestrial while breeding, but they winter at sea and thus also qualify. Some pelicans, grebes, ducks, loons and skimmers spend a great deal of time at sea, but none of these groups has marine representatives in southern Africa, so they are not considered here.

There are some 400 seabird species worldwide, representing 3.6% of the world's total bird species – yet they occupy over 70% of the world's surface. Despite their limited diversity, seabirds hold a special place in the hearts of many birders. Part of their attraction is the challenge they pose for humans, of getting to grips with a group of birds that is at home in one of the most inaccessible – and often hostile – habitats.

But seabirds also have a strong inherent appeal. They are the most mobile organisms on Earth, undertaking incredible migrations. Most species breed in impressive aggregations, commuting long distances between breeding sites and foraging areas. They breed in extreme habitats, ranging from Grey Gull colonies in the hot, arid wastes of the Atacama Desert, to the frigid Antarctic winter, where Emperor Penguins raise their chicks.

Penguins are particularly popular due to their erect stance, which gives them a superficial resemblance to people. Albatrosses rival humans in terms of longevity and are renowned for their long-term pair bonds. The truly pelagic species have become icons of one of the last habitats that bear few visible imprints of human activities, while some coastal seabirds such as the gulls are familiar commensals that have learned to adapt to the burgeoning human population.

Southern Africa and the adjacent Southern Ocean is a region blessed with a wealth of birds – close to 1,000 species occur in this region (almost 10% of all species worldwide), of which more than 100 are found nowhere else. Even more impressive

Seabird origins

All seabirds evolved from a single radiation of aquatic birds that diversified rapidly some 65 million years ago to fill the many vacant niches following the mass extinction event that saw the demise of all non-avian dinosaurs. Within this large group of waterbirds, termed the Aequorlitornithes, there are two major groupings. One, comprising the shorebirds, gulls, terns, skuas and alcids, has at its base the flamingos and grebes. The second group contains all other seabirds as well as the storks, herons, spoonbills and ibises, with the tropicbirds (together with the Sunbittern and Kagu) at its base.

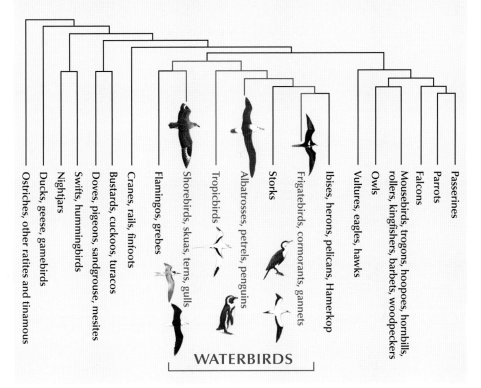

is the diversity of seabirds – 142 species have been recorded from the region, more than one-third of all seabirds, and 12 are breeding endemics. The region boasts all three species of tropicbirds, 86% of skuas, 77% of albatrosses, 61% of penguins, 60% of frigatebirds, 54% of terns, 50% of gannets and boobies, 44% of petrels/shearwaters and 34% of storm petrels. By comparison, gulls (21%) and cormorants (15%) are relatively poorly represented. The alcids and loons, which are confined to the northern hemisphere, are the only seabird families not found in the region. An

astounding nine seabird species have been added to the regional list since the first edition was published in 2017, indicating that seabirding is one of the most exciting birding activities.

A new feature of this second edition is the inclusion of flying fish and squid – amazing creatures that birders encounter in the warmer waters around southern Africa. Their addition will hopefully stimulate research on their distribution and abundance, as well as give birders something to look for in the long lean spells between bird sightings in the tropics!

Bird Island in Algoa Bay is home to the largest gannet colony in the world

THE OCEAN ENVIRONMENT

The main reason for the rich diversity of seabirds found off southern Africa and in the adjacent Southern Ocean is the varied and dynamic nature of the ocean in the region. Just as bird diversity on land depends in large part on the range of habitats in an area, so seabird diversity is dictated by a range of habitat niches at sea. Some species hug the coast to take advantage of productive coastal ecosystems, or because they cannot roost at sea (e.g. most cormorants). Others are truly oceanic, seldom visiting the continental shelf and only venturing close to land at their breeding islands. Within these broad categories, different seabirds have specific sea temperature preferences, which link directly to the availability of food.

Most marine food webs depend on microscopic phytoplankton – a rich cocktail of unicellular diatoms, dinoflagellates and photosynthetic bacteria that drift near the ocean surface. Primary production by these organisms requires nutrients such as nitrates and phosphates, and light. Because light is absorbed rapidly by water, most production is confined to within 20–50m of the sea surface. Shallow coastal waters are productive because they receive nutrients in run-off from land, and because the sea is shallow enough for phytoplankton to remain in the light.

Below 100m the ocean is a cold, dark realm that is rich in nutrients because there is little primary production to use them up. Oceanic phytoplankton rely on vertical mixing to bring nutrients close to the sea surface, where there is enough light for photosynthesis.

In tropical regions, surface waters are strongly stratified by solar heating, largely preventing nutrients from mixing up from deeper waters. Bacteria and tiny dinoflagellates dominate here, because their relatively large surface areas are efficient at scavenging the few nutrients available. These organisms are too small to support the short food chains that feed large numbers of seabirds;

furthermore seabirds face more competition from fish (see p. 9), so when birding in the tropics you can go hours without seeing a single bird. At the other extreme, polar seas are light limited in winter, but experience a spring bloom as light returns to their nutrient-rich surface waters, creating abundant food for seabirds that are ideally adapted to exploit seasonally predictable food concentrations.

Southern Africa's east coast is characterised by the warm Agulhas Current. This vast, fast stream of tropical water frequently spins off large anticyclonic eddies that carry heat into the South Atlantic as the flow turns back on itself, forming the Agulhas Return Current. Shear forces at the edges of these currents and eddies drive vertical mixing, bringing nutrients up from the depths and fuelling more primary production than is typical of most tropical waters.

By comparison, the oceanic circulation off the west coast is a more gentle northward drift associated with the South Atlantic Gyre. The frigid waters that characterise the west coast are often attributed to this northward flow, but surface waters in the gyre are a balmy 18–21°C. In fact, the cold waters along the west coast occur when southerly winds combine with the Coriolis force (deflection caused by the rotation of the Earth) to push surface waters offshore, creating a local drop in sea level. This is balanced by the upwelling of cold (8–12°C), nutrient-rich bottom water. As these waters warm, they support dense blooms of large-celled diatoms that feed the west coast's rich fisheries and make the region a Mecca for seabirds.

South of Africa, the Agulhas Return Current pushes south of 40°S, creating a particularly intense Subtropical Front and enhancing vertical mixing. Farther south still, primary production peaks at the sub-Antarctic and Antarctic Polar Fronts, which attract large congregations of prions and other seabirds. South Africa's Prince Edward Islands benefit from lying east of the Southwest Indian Ridge. Eddies form as the Antarctic Circumpolar Current passes over this ridge, increasing productivity and providing reliable feeding areas for the islands' many breeding birds.

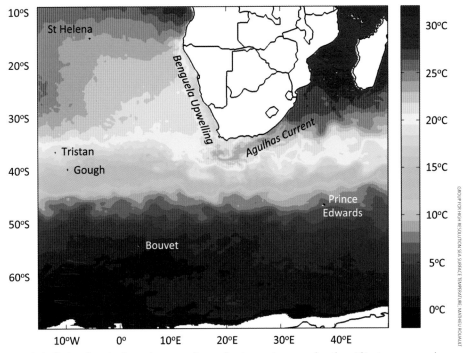

A strong latitudinal gradient dominates the pattern of sea surface temperature around southern Africa in summer, and contrasts with the warm Agulhas Current flowing down the east coast with cool inshore upwelling along the west coast

FEW SAFE HAVENS

In contrast to the wealth of marine habitats that sustain birds, breeding locations in southern Africa are limited, presenting a distinct handicap to seabirds in the region. There are only a handful of tiny inshore islands, scattered along the southern Namibian coast, off the Western Cape and in Algoa Bay. Offshore, islands are equally scarce – Europa Island in the Mozambique Channel is the sole tropical island; the Tristan da Cunha Archipelago and Gough Island in the central South Atlantic Ocean are the only cool temperate islands, and the Prince Edward Islands (including Marion Island) and Crozet Archipelago in the southwest Indian Ocean the only sub-Antarctic islands. Farther south, Bouvet is the most remote landmass on Earth, and beyond that the Dronning Maud Land coast of Antarctica offers few rocky areas for seabirds to breed. As a result, the few islands that exist support high densities of breeding seabirds (at least historically). A large proportion of our seabirds are non-breeding visitors that travel long distances to exploit the food-rich waters around southern Africa.

Cape Gannets breed at higher densities than other gannet species

The coast of southern Africa has not always had so few islands. Changes in sea level of up to 100m higher and lower than the current level over the last few million years has resulted in massive changes in the location and shape of the coastline, doubtless with marked consequences for seabirds breeding in the region. We have little information on seabird communities from colder periods when the sea level was much lower, as their former colonies are now under the sea, but we have a rich fossil record from warmer periods when sea levels were higher than they are today. The best data come from sediments along the west coast north of Cape Town that were laid down around 5 million years ago, when sea levels were about 90m higher than today, making islands of the Cape Peninsula and the Vredenburg area. Despite the relatively warm conditions at the time, many species we now consider to be confined to islands farther south bred in the area. These included at least two species of penguin (one of which was a large ancestor of the *Pygoscelis* penguins), three species of prion (the commonest being a giant species much larger than any extant species), a diving petrel and an albatross. Other seabirds appear to have been more typical of warmer waters, including a *Pelagodroma* storm petrel and a small booby. Their subsequent disappearance possibly resulted from a shortage of safe breeding islands once the sea level fell.

Back to the ocean

Seabirds and marine mammals (whales, dolphins, seals and sirenians) all evolved from terrestrial ancestors. They have many adaptations for a life at sea, but all remain air-breathing. This constrains them to return to the surface to breathe, limiting their ability to exploit life in the deep ocean. However, it's a necessary compromise because the concentration of dissolved oxygen in the ocean (<1%) is much less than in air (21%), and birds and mammals need lots of oxygen to maintain a constant body temperature. Endothermy gives these animals a huge advantage over cold-blooded fish and invertebrates at high latitudes. The maximum swimming speeds of ectotherms reduce with water temperature, making it much easier for seabirds and mammals to catch their prey in cold environments, which explains the dominance of seabirds and marine mammals as predators at high latitudes. Their advantage is greatly reduced in the tropics, where fish can have body temperatures – and swimming speeds – similar to those of penguins, seals and dolphins. Three factors combine to explain the scarcity of seabirds in the tropics: primary production is generally low in the strongly stratified surface waters, their prey is more agile, and there is more intense competition from predatory fish.

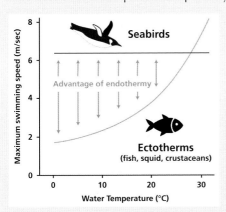

Marine endotherms (seabirds and marine mammals) swim much faster than ectotherms in cold water, giving them a huge competitive advantage (left), which explains the dominance of seabirds, seals and whales at higher latitudes, such as this crowded beach on Marion Island (right)

MAKING A LIVING

Seabirds are carnivores; some gulls are opportunistic scavengers on land where they might eat some plant material, but animals comprise all their food at sea. The main fare for almost all species is some combination of fish, squid, crustaceans and/or carrion, but a few species have more exotic tastes, eating planktonic salps, jellyfish, other invertebrates, and even other seabirds on occasion. Diet composition and diversity is determined in part by foraging methods.

Pursuit divers – whether wing-propelled, such as penguins and diving petrels, foot-propelled, such as cormorants, or a combination of the two, such as shearwaters – typically have more luxury to select their prey than do species that are confined to foraging close to the surface by either pattering (storm petrels) or surface-seizing (most albatrosses and petrels, gulls, skuas and some terns). Plunge divers (tropicbirds, gannets, boobies and most terns) tend to fall between these extremes, with the degree of dietary selectivity linked to the depth to which they dive.

Other, less common foraging methods include filter feeding (the larger-billed prions or 'whale-birds' have filtering lamellae lining the sides of their bills and large muscular tongues to pump water through these lamellae, trapping tiny copepods and other zooplankton) and piracy (best developed in the frigatebirds and skuas). Frigatebirds are unusual in lacking waterproof feathers, and so take all their food from the air.

Seabirds use a diversity of methods to locate their prey. Excellent vision is crucial for all species of birds in order to search for prey directly, or to cue in on the foraging activities of other species – both birds and other predators (e.g. seals, cetaceans, tunas, etc.). Many seabird prey species – small fish, squid and zooplankton – undergo daily vertical migrations, coming close to the surface at night and descending again during the day. As a result, some seabirds with limited diving abilities are crepuscular or even nocturnal. However, many surface feeders are opportunistic scavengers, eating prey that floats after dying. Squid, in particular, are short-lived, and those species that float when they are dead or dying feature strongly in the diets of many surface-seizing species, including most albatrosses and petrels.

African Penguins can dive down to 110m

Seabirds that cannot dive deeply, such as the Kelp Gull and Shy Albatross, tend to be generalist foragers and scavengers

Petrels have a well-developed sense of smell; these giant petrels, storm petrels, Wandering Albatrosses and a Cape Petrel have travelled hundreds of kilometres to feed on a dead Sperm Whale

At a larger spatial scale, scent can be important to locate productive areas in which to seek food. Many petrels and storm petrels have a keen sense of smell, and it is this trait that birders exploit when they 'chum' for petrels, laying a slick of fish oil on the water to attract these birds. Petrels also cue in on dimethyl sulphide (DMS), a chemical compound released when phytoplankton is grazed. African Penguins have also been shown to be attracted by DMS – which makes sense because their preferred prey, sardines, feed on large phytoplankton chains. The ability to locate prey at a distance is especially important for penguins because their commuting speed is appreciably slower than that of flying seabirds. Many petrels also use scent to find their nests: forced to come ashore after dark to reduce the risk of being killed by predatory skuas, they use their keen sense of smell to locate their nests among the myriad other burrows.

Hold the salt

Most seabird prey has the same salt concentration as seawater, which is three times more salty than bird tissues. Seabirds thus face the challenge of excreting a heavy salt burden without becoming dehydrated. Their kidneys are not up to the task, but most birds, along with many reptiles, have specialised glands located in depressions on the skull above the eye sockets. These salt glands strip sodium and chlorine ions from the blood and excrete a highly concentrated salt solution down ducts leading into the nostrils. This explains the drip of liquid often seen on the tips of seabird bills – they really do have a runny nose.

A drip of hypersaline liquid from a Spectacled Petrel's salt gland glistens on its bill tip

11

Dinner by candlelight

King Penguin eye showing tiny pupil

Light is absorbed rapidly by water, so it is very gloomy once you dive beyond 50 or 100m. Diving seabirds therefore dive mainly during daylight and go deepest in the middle of the day when light penetration is greatest. Their eyes have to cope with the massive difference in light levels between the surface and at the depths where they hunt their food. In vertebrate eyes, most of the accommodation to differing light levels results from chemical changes in the receptor cells of the retina. However, this takes time. When we go into a dark cinema we stumble around blindly, but after a few minutes we can see quite well. Most birds dive for only a few minutes, so cannot afford to rely on these relatively slow chemical changes. Instead, they have evolved a massive pupillary response. When our pupils are fully dilated they let in about eight times more light than when they are contracted; by contrast, penguins' and cormorants' pupils contract to tiny pinholes in daylight, but expand to let in up to 300 times more light when fully dilated.

SEABIRDS ON THE MOVE

Seabirds are the most mobile organisms on Earth – Arctic Terns undertake the longest of all migrations, travelling up to 100,000km annually, and the South Polar Skua is the only vertebrate other than humans to have reached the South Pole. The trans-equatorial migrations of seabirds easily rival those of their terrestrial counterparts. Among shearwaters alone, tens of millions of *Ardenna* shearwaters migrate from their southern breeding islands to winter in the northern hemisphere, while more modest numbers of northern-breeding *Calonectris* and Manx shearwaters winter in the south.

We have long been fascinated by seabirds' ability to navigate the seemingly featureless oceans. In a classic experiment in 1952, a Manx Shearwater breeding in Wales was flown almost 5,000km across the Atlantic to Boston. It arrived back at its colony 12 days later, having travelled at least 400km per day. It was able to work out where home was despite being bundled up in the hold of a commercial jet for its first trans-Atlantic crossing. Subsequently, Leach's Storm Petrels translocated from Canada to the UK displayed the same feat, covering the return journey of 4,750km in less than 14 days. Closer to home, Peter, Percy and Pamela, three African Penguins, attained fame when they were fitted with satellite transmitters to follow their movements after being trucked to Port Elizabeth to prevent them from being oiled by the *Treasure* shipwreck in 2000. All three unerringly headed west along the coast and arrived back off Cape

Town a few weeks later, along with thousands of their peers, after the oil had dispersed.

We now know that seabirds use a range of cues to navigate at sea. An elegant clock-shift experiment confirmed that shearwaters have a built-in clock that enables them to use the sun and stars to orient. They also learn to recognise landmarks such as headlands when in sight of land, and scent can play a role in navigation for some species.

Learning is also important. Gannets exploit most of the sea within 200–300km of their colonies, but individuals typically visit the same area within this zone, not only on successive trips, but over successive breeding seasons. Similarly, individuals tend to exhibit the same post-breeding dispersal patterns. For example, most Wandering

EGEVANG ET AL. 2010, PNAS

Migration paths of Arctic Terns breeding in Greenland: green = southbound; red = wintering area; yellow = northbound

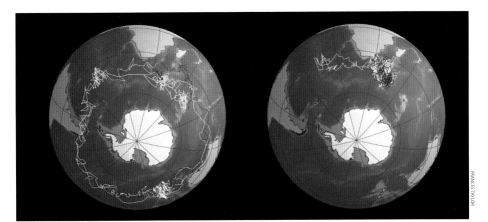

Between breeding attempts, some Wandering Albatrosses from Prince Edward Islands circle the Southern Ocean up to three times (left), but most remain in the Indian Ocean, or occasionally visit the Atlantic (right)

Albatrosses breeding on Marion Island remain in the Indian Ocean, occasionally venturing into the South Atlantic, but some make repeated circumnavigations of the Southern Ocean.

For long-distance migrants, their choice of wintering areas may be under genetic control. At one colony of Sabine's Gulls studied in Arctic Canada, a few birds winter in the Benguela off southern Africa, whereas most go to the Humboldt off western South America. Members of one pair that bred together for three years consistently wintered in different ocean basins – it would be fascinating to know where their offspring go. Red-necked Phalaropes also show abrupt changes in wintering areas – those breeding in Scandinavia winter in the Arabian Sea, whereas those from Scotland and Iceland fly across Central America to winter off Peru.

Tracking seabirds

For many years biologists could only speculate about the distance seabirds travelled while breeding or migrating. In the last few decades, however, a suite of devices has been developed to track their movements. Satellite transmitters send signals to a network of orbiting satellites; their main advantage is that they do not require the bird to be retrieved to find out where it has flown, but they are fairly large and expensive. GPS loggers use the commercial GPS satellite network to record a bird's position. They are very accurate, but unless the device is attached to a transmitting system (which adds mass and cost) the bird needs to be recaptured to obtain the data. The smallest, and longest-lasting devices are geolocators, simple light meters that use differences in day length to estimate latitude, and time of sunrise and sunset to estimate longitude. They weigh less than 1g, can run for several years, and allow us to track even the smallest of seabirds on their ocean wanderings. Once again the bird needs to be recaptured to obtain readings, and accuracy is crude (within only about 200km) so geolocators are useful only for birds that cover large distances.

A Wandering Albatross equipped with a GPS logger and 'daily diary' to track its movements

RAISING A FAMILY

Most birds are 'central place foragers' while breeding – commuting back and forth to their nests to incubate the eggs or feed the chicks. But seabirds take this to extremes. Some albatrosses and petrels commute thousands of kilometres from their oceanic breeding islands to forage in continental waters during incubation, and even when making relatively short foraging trips to provision young chicks, they still often travel more than 1,000km from their nests. Such long commutes take time, even for fast-flying seabirds, so prey is delivered to chicks only relatively infrequently. As a result, all seabirds (with the exception of polyandrous phalaropes, whose precocial chicks feed themselves) are monogamous (at least socially) – rearing chicks takes the efforts of both parents. In most cases, members of a pair remain together for successive years, because there is an advantage to working within an established partnership. There are some exceptions, though. King and Emperor penguins operate under tight time constraints when breeding and typically cannot afford to wait to see if their partner from the previous year is still alive; most form new pairings each year.

Even with the joint efforts of both parents, pelagic seabirds that feed far offshore can provision only a single chick and therefore lay only 1 egg. And even that single chick grows slowly. In the case of frigatebirds and some albatrosses, the breeding cycle lasts a year or even longer, limiting these species to raising a chick only every second year. Many long-

A Southern Giant Petrel cares for its chick

The flight-dive trade-off

Seabirds are among the best fliers on Earth. Albatrosses use the differential wind speed between wave troughs and crests to soar effortlessly at up to 120km/h, and young frigatebirds and Sooty Terns spend months aloft without ever landing. But aerial prowess comes at a cost – large wings suitable for dynamic soaring or gliding trap lots of air, limiting these birds to exploiting prey only very near the surface.

African Penguins underwater

Perhaps surprisingly, the air trapped in plumage is most problematic for birds foraging near the surface – as you dive deeper, the increasing water pressure compresses the air, reducing buoyancy. Most diving birds actively swim down when they are near the surface, but sink once they pass a certain depth. The opposite occurs on the way up – they have to swim to ascend until they pass the point of neutral buoyancy, from where they can ascend passively to surface. Cormorants reduce their buoyancy by having partly wettable plumage, decreasing the volume of air. This makes diving easier, but constrains most species to forage close to land because they cannot roost at sea. Because water is much denser than air, seabirds that use their wings to 'fly' underwater need smaller, stiffer wings. Shearwaters and diving petrels partly close their wings when diving, whereas penguins and the extinct Great Auk lost the ability to fly in air in order to become more efficient divers.

Delayed digestion

Caspian Tern with prey

When feeding chicks, most terns and some auks carry prey items in their beaks, and the diving petrels and some auklets have special gular sacs to transport food. But most seabirds carry their prey back to their nests in their stomach. This can be problematic when birds travel long distances between feeding and breeding areas. Seabirds' highly acidic digestive juices process most prey within a few hours. How do they avoid digesting all the food before they get back to their chicks? Albatrosses and petrels store much of their food as energy-rich stomach oil, which also serves as a defence mechanism. They can 'spit' this pungent oil several feet, deterring potential predators. Penguins have adopted a different strategy: they are able to 'turn off' their stomach, stopping peristalsis and making the pH neutral, storing food for days or even weeks. Male King Penguins, which undertake the last incubation shift, can store food for up to six weeks to feed to their newly hatched chicks. Male Emperor Penguins – who fast for up to four months over the incubation period – go one step further and feed their chicks an oil-rich secretion until their partner returns with fresh food.

A King Penguin feeds its chick
OTTO WHITEHEAD

distance commuters alternate between short and long foraging trips while feeding their chick. On the short trips, lasting only a few days each, they forage almost entirely for the chick, losing body mass in the process. After several short trips, they take a longer trip that lasts 1–2 weeks to replenish their own mass before once again collecting food for the chick. Another strategy is to take their chick to sea, and thus cut the commuting distance. Some auk chicks join their parents at sea within days of hatching, but the only southern African species that leans in this direction is the Damara Tern, which often takes its single chick to sheltered coastal waters as soon as it can flutter. However, the need to reduce the risk of predation by mammals scavenging along the coast is more likely the reason for this, rather than saving on the foraging commute.

Coupled with their slow reproductive rate, many seabirds also take a long time to mature. Making a living at sea requires a range of skills –

Some coastal terns such as Caspian Terns (left) can raise more than one chick, but Damara Terns (right) lay only a single egg

not only knowing how to catch prey, but also where it is most likely to be found. As a result, very few seabirds breed before they are two years old; 3–5 years is typical of many coastal species, and some pelagic species take 10 or more years before they breed for the first time. Many young seabirds fail to make the grade at all – typically, fewer than half of the fledglings that depart for sea survive to return as breeding adults. The combination of a low reproductive rate, delayed maturity, and a high risk of mortality before their first breeding attempt means that adults have to

live a long time – and thus raise numerous chicks – in order to maintain their populations.

In the absence of humans, this is achievable. Among the larger species, adult seabirds have few natural enemies and have high survival rates. We have not been studying seabirds long enough to know how long exceptional individuals live. 'Wisdom', the much-celebrated female Laysan Albatross who was ringed as a breeding adult on Midway Island, Hawaii, in 1956, is still raising chicks and must be close to 70 years old. Even much smaller petrels can

A Southern Giant Petrel chick's nest is ringed with guano, promoting the growth of nutrient-loving plants such as the grass *Poa cookii*

Millions of Macaroni Penguins have scored grooves in this rock

A Wandering Albatross defecates at sea

Nutrient transfer

Breeding as they do on land, seabirds are important vectors of nutrients and energy from marine ecosystems to their breeding islands. At Marion Island alone, some 2 million breeding seabirds bring 4,500 tonnes of faeces and 600 tonnes of feathers, eggshells and carcasses ashore each year. This affects the types of plants that grow there by changing the nutrient status of the soils. Trampling and digging also affect vegetation composition and structure. In extreme cases, birds erode the surface down to bedrock, even scoring the rock with their claws over the millennia. At dry locations, such as the islands off the west coast of southern Africa, seabird deposits accumulate as guano, an excellent fertiliser that is rich in nitrogen and phosphorous. In Antarctica, the cold, dry conditions preserve the oily regurgitations that Snow Petrels use to defend themselves, so that the entrances to nest crevices slowly accumulate deep crusts of 'mumiyo'. At Robertskollen, near South Africa's SANAE base, mumiyo deposits date back more than 20,000 years.

A Grey-headed Albatross regurgitates a meal of squid to its large chick; the chick receives only one or two meals each week

achieve impressive ages – a Manx Shearwater has reached 55 and a Leach's Storm Petrel 36 years. The oldest known frigatebird attained 43 years, and other seabird families all have representatives that reached their thirties.

Such longevity records are sensitive to the numbers of birds ringed; and to reveal truly impressive ages, ringing studies have to be maintained for decades. It would not be surprising if long-term studies of Wandering Albatrosses start recording birds close to the century mark. However, in reality, only a very few Wandering Albatrosses live past 40. By the time they turn 30, most show some evidence of reduced fecundity and, although there is little evidence of physiological deterioration, older birds typically have to work harder to find food for their chicks than birds in their prime reproductive years. However, the mechanisms underlying their senescence are not well understood.

Coastal birds have less extreme life histories than oceanic seabirds. By foraging closer to their breeding sites, coastal seabirds can deliver more food to their nests, which allows them to rear more chicks and thus lay larger clutches of eggs. Cormorants – which feed close to home due to their partly wettable plumage – have the shortest foraging trips, and thus the largest clutches, of up to 7 eggs. But 2 or 3 eggs is the norm, even for coastal-breeding species. The combination of obligatory monogamy, small clutch sizes and delayed maturity is so typical of seabirds that it is known as the 'seabird syndrome'.

A Bank Cormorant with its family of three downy chicks

17

MOULT

Breeding is a stressful time for birds, but it can be deferred if conditions are unfavourable or delayed until birds have learned how to survive at sea. By comparison, moult is something that all birds must do in order to survive. Feathers are crucial for flight and insulation, provide physical protection and waterproofing, and determine a bird's appearance. However, they are dead structures and once grown, they start to deteriorate through abrasion, UV radiation, fungi, bacteria and ectoparasites such as feather mites. Preening feathers and coating them in preen gland oil helps to slow their rate of wear, but they must be replaced regularly. Moulting involves the growth of new feathers, which push out the old ones. But moult is more than just plumage replacement; it is linked to widespread tissue renovation and results in changes in blood volume, water turnover and bone metabolism. It is thus a stressful time for birds, and typically is not undertaken during breeding or migrating.

One strategy to limit the time that birds are affected by moulting is to replace all flight feathers at once, rendering the birds temporarily flightless (e.g. some diving petrels and auks). Penguins take this to the extreme by replacing all their feathers at once, coming ashore and fasting for 3–4 weeks. But most seabirds need to retain the ability to fly, and thus have to juggle moulting with other key events in their annual cycle. Scheduling flight-feather moult is particularly challenging for large birds, because the rate of feather growth is more or less constant irrespective of bird size. It thus takes a large bird much longer to grow a primary feather than it does a small bird.

Giant petrels are the largest birds that replace all their primaries each year and still retain the ability to fly. They achieve this feat by starting to moult while breeding (especially the larger males), and by moulting a large number of primaries at once, creating a distinctive gap in the wing during the early stages of primary moult. However, they do not usually replace all secondaries each year, as do several other large petrels. Albatrosses, which have the longest of all wings, typically only replace a subset of primaries each year, and may take up to 3–4 years to fully replace all their secondaries. The number of flight feathers adults grow each year depends on the time available between breeding attempts. Gannets and cormorants reduce the impact of moulting several primaries at once by having multiple active moult centres that work slowly across the wing (wave moult).

Feathers are dead structures that have to be replaced every year or so, or they will deteriorate to the point where they no longer function for flight or insulation; this unfortunate Crowned Cormorant has not moulted its wings for several years, and is close to becoming unable to fly

Blue Petrels moult their wings in Antarctic waters shortly after breeding, replacing up to 7 primaries and all their greater coverts at once

Kelp Gulls replace all their greater coverts at the start of wing moult, allowing them to moult large numbers of secondaries once the new coverts are grown

Moult can affect the flight action and appearance of birds, and needs to be considered as a factor if birds show odd plumage features. For example, many species show white wing bars while moulting their wing coverts, which exposes the pale bases of the underlying feathers. However, moult patterns can assist with identification if similar species moult at different times of year (e.g. some prions moult immediately after breeding, whereas others moult later in winter). However, immature seabirds often moult earlier than adults because they are not constrained by the breeding season. Moult also can be useful for ageing albatrosses. The great albatrosses and mollymawks typically alternate moulting inner and outer primaries in successive years, starting with the outer 3 primaries in year 2.

Most albatrosses alternate moulting their inner and outer primaries, but some, such as this Indian Yellow-nosed Albatross, can have more complex moults, retaining some primaries for more than 2 years

Things that go bump in the night

Diving species such as penguins, cormorants, gannets and terns forage almost exclusively by day. At night they either roost ashore (e.g. coastal species such as cormorants and most terns) or on the water if they are too far from their colonies to commute home (e.g. penguins and gannets). However, for surface-feeding species, such as many albatrosses and petrels, the night is the time to feed. Many small fish and zooplankton undergo a vertical migration each day to reduce the risk of predation, moving close to the surface at night, then descending into the depths during the day. However, seabirds typically need some light to see their prey, and so they tend to be most active at dawn and dusk. Many geolocators contain a simple salt-water switch that records when seabirds sit on the water. These devices have provided fascinating insights into seabird activity at night.

Most albatrosses and petrels fly more during the day than at night, although they can fly all night when moving between preferred foraging areas or commuting to and from their colonies while breeding. They tend to show a marked response to lunar cycles, foraging at night mainly when the moon is full. Stomach temperature loggers show that Wandering Albatrosses obtain about 10% of their food at night – typically smaller squid than those they scavenge during the day. Recent studies suggest that by swimming in circles at night, albatrosses stimulate bioluminescent organisms to light up, luring squid to the surface.

Sooty Albatross

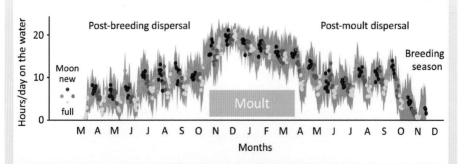

Seasonal changes in activity patterns (hours per day sitting on the water) recorded by geolocator loggers attached to the legs of non-breeding Sooty Albatrosses at Marion Island (from Schoombie *et al.* 2022, *Polar Biology* 45: 31–44). Successful breeders take a year off between breeding attempts, and moult their flight feathers in the summer of their sabbatical year. Outside the moult period, they show distinct activity cycles linked to moon phase, being more active at full than new moon.

SEABIRD CONSERVATION

A consequence of seabirds' low reproductive rates and delayed maturity is that they cannot cope with much unnatural mortality arising from human activities. This fact, together with their reliance on two habitats – land for breeding and sea for foraging – renders many seabirds susceptible to human impacts. Roughly one-third of all seabirds are threatened with extinction, an appreciably higher proportion than for birds on average. The conservation status of seabirds has deteriorated faster than that of almost any other group of birds over the last few decades.

Most seabirds breed on islands and sea cliffs to avoid the attentions of terrestrial predators. As humans spread around the planet, and especially as they reached oceanic islands for the first time, they caused havoc for the many organisms that had evolved there. More than 90% of all bird extinctions in the last 500 years have been of species confined to oceanic islands. Several of these were seabirds, including two species of petrels on St Helena, which lies just outside our area of interest.

Seabirds suffered initially as they were hunted for food, with adults, chicks and eggs all targeted. In South Africa alone, more than 100,000 African Penguin eggs were collected each year in the first part of the 20th century – little wonder penguin numbers decreased massively over this period. Albatrosses and petrels that winter off the Cape were also caught for food by fishers. Malmok (mollymawk) and basiaan (White-chinned Petrel) were regularly sold at Cape Town markets up to the 1950s, and illegal killing was still common at least until the 1980s. Fortunately, seabirds and their breeding islands are now protected throughout most of the region, although some birds are still killed for food or to prevent them from stealing bait from line fisheries.

These days, the main issues for seabirds on land are introduced predators. House Mice, introduced inadvertently by early sealing parties, kill tens of thousands of albatross and petrel chicks each year on Gough Island. And on Marion Island, cats introduced to keep mice out of the South African weather station in 1949 soon turned feral. By the 1970s some 2,000 cats were killing 450,000 seabirds each year, causing at least one species to disappear from the island entirely. Fortunately, a sustained campaign to remove the cats finally succeeded in 1991, but mice remain on the island and in recent years have also started killing large numbers of albatross and petrel chicks. The good news is that predators can be removed from islands – even rats and mice. Sadly, the attempt to eradicate mice from Gough

Seabirds breeding on islands are particularly vulnerable to introduced predators; on Marion Island, House Mice attack and often kill Grey-headed and Wandering albatross chicks (inset)

Oil pollution affects mainly penguins, such as this Northern Rockhopper Penguin at Tristan da Cunha

Island in 2021 failed, but South Africa is currently raising funds to tackle mice on Marion Island.

The main threats at sea these days are pollution and interactions with fisheries. Oil pollution is a highly visible threat – especially during major spills – but each year hundreds of seabirds are oiled due to smaller, less publicised spillages. Rehabilitation centres can treat the symptoms of oiling, especially for penguins, provided this is done promptly. However, cleaned birds breed less often and less successfully than those never oiled, so prevention is definitely better than cure.

Seabirds also obtain a potentially lethal cocktail of heavy metals, pesticides and other persistent organic pollutants through their food. Long-lasting pollutants from land tend to end up in the oceans, and many accumulate in top predators such as seabirds. Plastics are a particularly visible form of this pollution, and many seabirds off southern Africa eat plastic items, either accidentally with their food or by mistaking them for prey items. Having a stomach full of plastic reduces the space available for food, and plastics also carry a variety of toxic compounds into the birds.

But for most seabirds the most serious threat comes from fishing operations. Tens of thousands of seabirds are killed accidentally by fishing gear each year. Gill nets are most lethal, but they are seldom used in our region. Long-line fisheries also kill large numbers of birds – mainly albatrosses and large petrels, but also gannets, skuas and even penguins – when these birds attempt to steal bait from the hooks. A variety of mitigation measures have reduced the impact of these fisheries, but the vessels targeting tunas and swordfish remain a problem, especially in international waters. The trawl cables of the hake fishery were also killing

Before bird-scaring lines were introduced, many albatrosses were drowned when their long wings were entangled in trawl cables, dragging the birds underwater

Long-line fisheries for tuna and swordfish still kill large numbers of seabirds, mainly albatrosses and large petrels

Climate change exacerbates many of the threats facing seabirds; during hot weather, African Penguins cool down by panting and have to abandon their nests in order to drink if the heat persists

large numbers of birds attracted to scavenge behind fishing vessels, but this problem has been largely solved by deploying bird-scaring lines to keep birds away from the danger zone.

A more difficult issue is where fisheries and birds compete for the same prey. The purse seine fishery for sardines caused the collapse of small pelagic fish stocks off Namibia in the 1970s, resulting in a massive increase in jellyfish and salps. These species mop up most eggs and larvae produced by the few remaining fish, preventing any recovery to a fish-dominated ecosystem. The crash in fish populations saw a corresponding collapse in populations of African Penguins, Cape Gannets and Cape Cormorants. Namibia, once the heart of the Benguela Upwelling region, now supports less than 20% of the region's breeding seabirds.

Sardine stocks also collapsed off the South African coast, but were replaced by anchovy. This allowed the seabirds that depend on small pelagic fish to persist, albeit at lower numbers than before the advent of industrial fishing. Judicious management of commercial fishing saw sardine stocks recover to some extent in the 1990s – a trend first detected through monitoring Cape Gannet diets. However, environmental changes towards the end of the 20th century, coupled with persistent fishing pressure mainly along the west coast, have led to a shift in pelagic fish stocks to the south coast where there are few breeding islands for seabirds. The African Penguin population has fallen by 70% in the last

20 years, and numbers of Cape Gannets and Cape Cormorants have also decreased dramatically, especially along the west coast. Measures are needed to ensure that fishery catches match the distribution of fish, and do not keep hammering the already depressed west coast populations. Bird Island in Algoa Bay now supports over 70% of the world's Cape Gannets, and until recently Bird and St Croix Islands together supported over half of the African Penguins. Sadly, penguin numbers in Algoa Bay have fallen by 60% in just the last five years, at least in part linked to the ill-advised use of the bay for ship-to-ship fuel transfers, which has led to numerous oil spills.

But it is not all doom and gloom. Seabird populations are resilient and can recover if given the chance to do so. Just imagine the upheaval caused during the 'white gold rush' of the 1850s, when work gangs from up to 20 ships competed to mine the guano from southern Africa's west coast islands. And yet penguins, gannets and cormorants survived. Spectacled Petrels were almost wiped out by introduced pigs on Inaccessible Island, Tristan da Cunha, but fortunately the pigs died out before they ate the last petrels. Today the petrel population grows by 7% per year, despite birds being killed on long-lines off South America. And even that icon of the oceans, the Wandering Albatross, is holding its own in the African sector of the Southern Ocean. More than 40% of the world population breeds at South Africa's Prince Edward Islands, where its numbers are stable.

A pair of Macaroni Penguins, each equipped with a satellite transmitter, greet each other before heading to sea for the winter

Indicators of ocean health

Seabirds are among the best-studied groups of birds. This is partly because all seabirds have to return to land to breed, where they are often quite approachable, and their dense breeding aggregations allow ornithologists to collect large amounts of data quickly. These traits make them ideal organisms on which to test a range of biological theories. However, seabirds are also valuable indicators of the general health of marine ecosystems. Tracking their diet, breeding success and population trends gives a more accurate picture of ocean health than is possible by attempting to monitor populations of fish, squid or crustacean prey. Measuring the effort parents take to find food for their chicks provides an independent assessment of fish stocks, which can be used to inform the sustainable management of fisheries.

WATCHING SEABIRDS

Coastal seabirds are fairly easy to observe. Most cormorants, gulls and terns forage along the coast and can be observed from land. Roost sites are particularly productive places to observe a range of these species, which often roost communally at protected river mouths or rock stacks.

Pelagic seabirds pose more of a challenge. Some species can be seen from the shore, typically from headlands, where they tend to pass close to land. Cape Gannets and some of the more common inshore pelagics such as White-chinned Petrels, Sooty Shearwaters and Shy Albatrosses are often visible from promontories, but you need a spotting scope to get even a half decent view. During stormy weather, more exotic species might be glimpsed from the shore. Winter gales at Cape Point and tropical cyclones along the east coast are most exciting, although potentially perilous for birders and seabirds alike.

But to really get to grips with pelagic seabirds you need to visit their realm, which means going to sea. Southern Africa's open coastline makes venturing to sea a tricky, and all too often a seasick-inducing event. Despite this, small-boat pelagic trips are popular, with Cape Town and Durban the major centres. Cape Town trips require

travelling farther out to sea – usually 40–50km off Cape Point – but the rewards are bigger in terms of numbers and diversity of birds. Several operators run trips, but they are weather dependent (Cape pelagics, in particular, are prone to cancellation), and even when the weather is passable, it is often rough enough to throw spray over the boats – make sure you are properly equipped (see checklist).

Another option is to go on a large vessel, which obviates many of the discomforts and vagaries of working from a small boat, but options are more limited and this mode of transport normally precludes the possibility of stopping to view birds, let alone chasing after interesting individuals. Also, most birds are intimidated by large ships, so it is nowhere near as intimate an experience as being in the heart of a large flock gathered behind a fishing boat. One advantage of larger vessels is that they are more stable, making it much easier to

Checklist for small-boat pelagics

❑ Anti-nausea drugs (taken in time to be effective)
❑ Sunscreen (reapply frequently)
❑ Sunhat and sunglasses
❑ Non-slip shoes
❑ Cold-weather gear (jumper, beanie, scarf, gloves)
❑ Waterproof outer wear
❑ Waterproof bag for camera (with padding)
❑ Snacks and drinks

Birders aboard a small ski boat enjoy the petrels and albatrosses gathered in the wake of a fishing boat off Cape Point

Thousands of petrels gather behind a trawler

Headland watches sometimes yield good birds

Photographing seabirds

Seabirds at sea can be tricky to photograph. Here are a few tips:

- Be aware of salt spray. Have a waterproof bag handy for use if conditions deteriorate.
- Small boats are often too unstable for really long telephoto lenses. A midrange zoom (100–500mm) is often a better bet.
- Use a predictive focusing mode. If you don't have animal-eye focusing, a single focus point can work better than multiple points, especially for birds flying against the sea.
- Exposure is tricky when photographing light and dark birds against the sea on a sunny day. Try shooting in manual exposure rather than changing the exposure compensation.
- Expect many bad shots, so take lots of pictures!

use binoculars. You can compensate for birds not coming as close by scanning the water ahead of the ship with binoculars. When birding in the tropics, you also need to look upwards for birds; tropicbirds and frigatebirds may drop down from above, circle the ship a few times, and then drift away.

Finally, you can observe and study seabirds at their breeding colonies. This tends to be the best approach for penguins, which are difficult to detect at sea (except in the Antarctic, where penguins obligingly sit on ice floes). African Penguins are best observed at Boulders, near Simon's Town, and Stony Point, Betty's Bay. The Cape Gannet colony at Bird Island, Lambert's Bay, is the town's main tourist attraction. Cormorants breed at several accessible sites, including Cape Point cliffs and Stony Point. Robben Island has a Bank Cormorant colony as well as breeding penguins, gulls and Greater Crested Terns, although these attractions do not feature on regular prison tours. All other southern African offshore islands are provincial or national reserves and can be visited only with special permission.

First prize is to be able to visit the sub-Antarctic or Antarctic breeding colonies. Unfortunately, tourism is not allowed to the Prince Edward Islands, and there are few, if any, tourist trips to Antarctica south of Africa, where Emperor Penguins are common. Most birders have to settle for a trip to the Antarctic Peninsula region, ideally linking with the Falklands/Malvinas and South Georgia. One exciting option is to join end-of-season repositioning cruises, which start near Cape Horn and cross the South Atlantic to Cape Town, visiting Tristan da Cunha and Gough Island en route.

HOW TO USE THIS BOOK

The book is arranged by seabird families. Each family starts with a brief introduction that highlights the main features of the family. The species accounts follow, with either a full or half page per species depending on the range of plumages that need to be depicted and the species' abundance in the region. Identification requires reference to the photographs, text and range maps.

Distribution maps

The maps summarise the areas where a species might be encountered, with the darker tone indicating where it is more common. However, seabirds are notoriously mobile, so the ranges are indicative rather than definitive. Green ranges show where species are present year-round, red where they are found mainly in summer, and blue mainly in winter.

	common	uncommon
resident		
summer visitor		
winter visitor		

species that irrupt north of their normal range in some years

✗ vagrant   breeding island

The species accounts highlight key identification features, describe the species' calls (under 'Voice'), and record various aspects of the bird's status, preferred habitat and biology. The accounts briefly describe the main plumages and highlight the most important characters for separating the species in question from similar species. Adult plumages are described first (male then female), followed by juvenile (first year) and immature plumages (second year and older), if these are distinct. For species with seasonal plumage differences, breeding plumage is usually described first, except where breeding plumage is very short-lived (e.g. some cormorants) or where non-breeding plumage is the norm in southern Africa (e.g. Palearctic migrant phalaropes, jaegers, gulls and terns).

'Status and biology' reports the global conservation status, abundance of each species globally and in the region, its movements, habitat preferences, breeding biology and diet. Breeding biology is given only for species that breed in the region. Abundance categories within the region are, in descending order: 'abundant', 'common', 'fairly common', 'uncommon', 'scarce', 'rare' and 'vagrant'. 'Locally common' is used for species with a restricted distribution (either in terms of specific habitat requirements or absolute range size).

Abbreviations used

ad – adult   sub-ad – sub-adult
imm – immature   juv – juvenile
br – breeding   non-br – non-breeding
sthn – southern   nthn – northern
N, S, W, E – north, south, west, east

Oceanic Islands

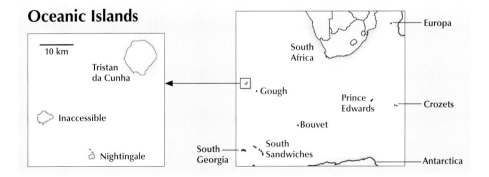

27

Macaroni and King penguins live cheek-by-jowl at Kildalkey Bay on Marion Island

PENGUINS

The extreme modification of penguins' body form led early biologists to assume that penguins formed a distinct lineage. We now know that they are the closest living relatives to the albatrosses and petrels, although the 2 groups diverged more than 60 million years ago. The 19 species in 6 genera, all confined to the southern hemisphere, range in size from the Little Penguin (~1kg) to the Emperor Penguin (up to 30kg). Historically, there were more species, with some weighing up to 100kg. Although Africa is currently home to only one breeding penguin, at least 4 species lived on the west coast 3–4 million years ago, apparently the result of multiple colonisation events.

Penguins have given up flight in order to become specialist pursuit divers. In water, which is much denser than air, their wings are needed only for propulsion, not lift. Their small, rigid flippers, which lack the large flight feathers found on the wings of all other seabirds, are ideal for 'flying' underwater, and trap little air, reducing buoyancy. Their buoyancy is further decreased by their solid bones and their habit of swallowing stones. Their feet are set far back on the body and, together with the tail and bill, used primarily for steering. These birds stand erect on land, sometimes aided by the stiff tail feathers.

Diving performance increases with body size. King Penguins regularly dive to >300m and Emperors to >500m, with dives lasting up to 22 minutes. Most dives are too short to cause problems with the 'bends', when nitrogen absorbed by the blood at depth forms tiny bubbles in the bloodstream if the body surfaces too rapidly. King and Emperor penguins surface gradually after deep dives, possibly to avoid this problem. Heat-exchange systems in the flippers and feet help to reduce heat loss from their extremities. Antarctic species further limit heat loss by having smaller bills and flippers than species living farther north.

The sexes look alike, but males average slightly larger. Juveniles have distinct plumages, which are replaced in the first complete moult. Penguins moult all their feathers simultaneously, coming ashore for 3–4 weeks and living off stored reserves. Moult duration scales with body size; larger species take longer to replace their feathers.

All penguins are socially monogamous and breed colonially. Clutch size typically is 1 or 2 eggs. Most penguins breed in scrapes, burrows or in rock crevices, but *Aptenodytes* penguins incubate their single egg balanced precariously on their feet. The sexes share incubation duties, although Emperor Penguins are an exception. The male bird cares for the egg from shortly after it is laid for 3 months through the bleak Antarctic winter until spring, when the chick hatches and the female returns from the sea. Penguin chicks are semi-altricial and are fed by regurgitation by both parents, although in *Eudyptes* penguins the female does all foraging during the brood-guard phase. Once juvenile penguins go to sea they receive no further assistance from their parents. After breeding, adults go on a pre-moult foraging trip when they accumulate sufficient reserves to carry them

through the moult fast. Thereafter some species migrate away from their breeding grounds.

Of the 18 penguin species recognised by the IUCN, nine are globally threatened and 3 Near Threatened. The main threats include competition with fisheries for food, pollution, and disturbance of their breeding grounds. Penguins, being flightless, are particularly susceptible to oil pollution. The African Penguin is Endangered; its population is less than 5% of what it was a century ago, and its numbers have more than halved over the last 20 years.

CLIFF DORSE

Emperor Penguins can dive to more than 500m

JOHN GRAHAM

Adelie Penguins are largely restricted to icy Antarctic waters

African Penguin *Spheniscus demersus*

60–70cm; 2.2–3.8kg

Ad has conspicuous black-and-white coloration on face, breast and flanks, which enhances prey capture by causing fish to panic and form dense 'bait balls'. Some individuals have 2 breast bands like Magellanic Penguins, but where this occurs the upper band is narrower and the bird lacks a pink line extending to base of bill. Juv lacks bold patterning, varying from greyish-blue when newly fledged to brown above as feathers wear. Some juvs moult part or all of their heads to ad plumage before their first complete moult, which allows them access to adult feeding groups at sea. **Voice:** Loud, donkey-like braying at colonies, especially at night. **Status and biology:** ENDANGERED; population has decreased by more than 70% over the last 20 years, mainly due to competition with fisheries for food. Breeding endemic; 16,000 pairs breed at 22 colonies from Hollams Bird Island, central Namibia, to Bird Island, Algoa Bay, with 3 regional populations: sthn Namibia (5,000 pairs), W Cape (7,000 pairs) and Algoa Bay (4,000 pairs). Most forage within 20km of land; rare >50km offshore; ads provisioning chicks have to locate sufficient food within 20–30km of colonies. Breeds year-round; least during peak moult period (Oct–Dec in most of range). Lays 1 or 2 eggs (rare 3-egg clutches possibly laid by more than one female) in a burrow, rock crevice or under vegetation; some pairs attempt 2 broods in a year. Ads largely sedentary at Algoa Bay colonies, but W Cape birds disperse up the west coast or onto the Agulhas Bank when not breeding. Juvs from W Cape colonies migrate north to Namibia. Feeds during the day, diving to 110m (max 4.5 minutes), but most dives <40m. Ads eat pelagic fish (mostly anchovies and sardines, but also round herrings, pelagic gobies, horse mackerel, squid); juvs target slower-moving fish. Prey usually swallowed underwater. Brilpikkewyn

Ad is variably spotted on underparts

Ad bold plumage is striking at sea

Ad with double breast band (uncommon)

Juvs (left) are much duller, although some undergo a partial head moult (centre) before moulting into ad plumage (right)

Magellanic Penguin *Spheniscus magellanicus*   70–76cm; 3.0–5.2kg

Slightly larger than African Penguin, with 2 breast bands; upper band broader; in African Penguins with 2 breast bands (uncommon) the upper band is typically incomplete or narrower than the lower band. Juv similar to juv African Penguin, but has a more patterned head and breast, with a faint pink line from eye to base of bill and a pale stripe under the base of the lower mandible. **Voice:** Braying call, similar to that of African Penguin. **Status and biology:** 1.3 million pairs breed from central Chile to Patagonia and the Falklands/Malvinas; migrate north as far as S Brazil. Rare vagrant to sthn Africa; one record in Cape Town harbour was probably ship-assisted, but vagrants have reached Tristan da Cunha and Marion Island. Eats mainly pelagic fish; dives to 100m (max 4.5 minutes). Magellaanse Pikkewyn

Ads have a broad upper breast band and black facial skin

Juv on Marion Island

Little Penguin *Eudyptula minor*   40–45cm; 700–1,600g

Diminutive penguin, resembling a tiny, recently fledged African Penguin, but has pale, creamy-grey (not dark grey) feet, plain face with no bare facial skin, a smaller, weaker bill, and eyes usually paler. The divide between blue-grey upperparts and white underparts better defined than in juv African Penguin. **Voice:** Loud growls and groans at colonies at night. **Status and biology:** Some 300,000 pairs breed in South Australia and New Zealand. Rare vagrant to sthn Africa; one record from Ichaboe Island, Namibia, Apr 2005. Eats small fish and squid. Kleinpikkewyn

Ads are largely nocturnal at their colonies

At sea, Little Penguins resemble tiny juv African Penguins

31

Northern Rockhopper Penguin *Eudyptes moseleyi*   48–58cm; 2.2–3.2kg

A fairly small penguin with a short, stubby, red bill and yellow crest that starts just in front of the eye; crests do not extend across forehead (compare Macaroni Penguin p.34). Ad has much longer and more luxuriant head plumes than in Eastern Rockhopper, more extensive black on the under-flipper and lacks the pink line along the base of the bill. Juv browner above, with a dull red bill; yellow crest reduced or absent, but has peaked crown feathers; separable from Eastern Rockhopper only by its darker under-flipper pattern. **Voice:** Deep, raucous *'kerr-aak, kerr-aak kerrak kerrak-kerrak-kerrak'* at colonies. Sometimes gives a soft honking call at sea. **Status and biology: ENDANGERED.** 250,000 pairs breed on Tristan da Cunha and Gough, Amsterdam and St Paul islands; 90% at Tristan and Gough, where numbers have decreased greatly over the last 50 years but numbers are currently fairly stable. Non-br ads from Gough Island disperse mainly from 35–50°S, between 15°W and 10°E. Regular vagrant to sthn Africa, mostly moulting juvs Nov–Mar. Breeds in spring, coming ashore in early Sept, 6 weeks earlier than Eastern Rockhopper Penguin; chicks fledge in mid-Jan. Most colonies at Tristan are hidden under dense tussock grass, but it breeds in the open on Gough Island. Lays 2 eggs, but raises only 1 chick, usually from larger, second-laid egg. Eats crustaceans, small fish and squid; dives to 168m (4 minutes), although most dives are 20–50m. **Noordelike Geelkuifpikkewyn**

Ad showing dark under-flipper

Ad's extravagant head plumes

Juv showing dark under-flipper

Eastern Rockhopper Penguin *Eudyptes filholi* 45–55cm; 1.8–2.8kg

Slightly smaller than Northern Rockhopper; ad has shorter crest and less extensive dark tips to under-flippers. Appreciably smaller than Macaroni Penguin (p.34), with narrow pink line around base of bill (not a large pink gape) and gold crests not meeting across the forehead. Juv separable from juv Northern Rockhopper only by its paler under-flipper pattern. **Voice:** Harsh '*kerr-ik kerrik kerik-kerik-kerik-kerik*', slightly higher-pitched than call of Northern Rockhopper Penguin. **Status and biology:** VULNERABLE globally, but ENDANGERED in South Africa. Recently split from the Southern Rockhopper *E. chrysocome*, which breeds at the Falklands/Malvinas and sthn S America. Some 420,000 pairs breed at sub-Antarctic islands in the Indian Ocean and south of New Zealand. 100,000 pairs breed at the Prince Edward Islands, where numbers have decreased by about 60% over the last few decades. Rare vagrant to sthn Africa, mainly Jan–Apr when birds come ashore to moult. Feeds fairly close to Marion Island when provisioning chicks, but travels some 700km south during the pre-moult fattening trip, foraging in 3–4°C water. During winter disperses over a large area from 43–55°S and 10–52°E. Breeds in loose colonies in summer, but several weeks later than larger Macaroni Penguins to reduce competition; returns to Marion Island in late Oct; chicks fledge in Mar. Agile on land, coming ashore on exposed sites; some colonies extend up to 250m on steep sea cliffs. Lays 2 eggs, but raises only 1 chick, usually from the larger, second-laid egg. Eats crustaceans, small fish and squid; dives to 113m (4 minutes), although most dives are 20–50m. Oostelike Geelkuifpikkewyn

Ad showing pale under-flipper

Ad's modest head plumes and pink line around lower bill

Ad porpoising

Juv showing pale under-flipper

Macaroni Penguin *Eudyptes chrysolophus*

68–75cm; 3.1–5.5kg

Larger than rockhopper penguins (pp.32–33), with a massive bill, broad pink gape and golden crest extending across forehead (although not obvious at sea). Some birds at Marion Island have white face with yellow wash around base of bill, resembling Royal Penguin, *E. schlegeli*, from Macquarie Island (which recent genetic studies indicate is just a form of Macaroni Penguin). Juv duller, with little or no crest. **Voice:** Deep, exultant braying at colonies; occasional '*harr*' at sea. **Status and biology: VULNERABLE.** 6.3 million pairs breed at sub-Antarctic islands, with the largest populations at the Crozet and Kerguelen islands; 270,000 pairs breed at the Prince Edward Islands, where numbers have decreased by almost 40% over the last 2 decades. Rare vagrant to South Africa; mainly moulting birds Feb–Apr. Feeds mainly in Antarctic waters year-round. After breeding, birds from Marion Island travel some 900km south for their pre-moult fattening trip, foraging in 3–4°C water. During winter they disperse from 47–61°S, 8–50°E, often feeding close to the sea-ice edge. Breeds in dense colonies in summer; returns to the islands in early Oct and fledges chicks at the end of Feb. Less agile on land than rockhopper penguins, but some colonies extend up to 200m on steep sea cliffs. Lays 2 eggs, but raises only 1 chick, usually from larger, second-laid egg. Eats crustaceans, small fish and squid; dives to 163m (7 minutes), although most dives are 20–50m.

Langkuifpikkewyn

Ad; note prominent pink gape

At sea, head plumes are plastered down and hard to see

White-faced form (Marion Island) resembles Royal Penguin

Juv showing dull bill and short crest

Gentoo Penguin *Pygoscelis papua* — 75–80cm; 4.2–7.2kg

The third-largest penguin; elegant and long-tailed with distinctive white flecking above its eyes and narrow white eye-rings. Feet and bill orange. Flippers long, with pale orange wash on underside. Juv has paler throat and smaller white 'ear' patches. **Voice:** Loud cawing at colonies. **Status and biology:** 390,000 pairs; not threatened globally thanks to its increasing population at the south of its range, but **ENDANGERED** in South Africa, with 1,500 pairs at the Prince Edward Islands. Very rare vagrant to South Africa. Breeds in summer in Antarctica (to 65°S in Antarctic Peninsula); mainly in winter or spring in the sub-Antarctic, but occasionally still on eggs in midsummer. Northern populations usually remain close to breeding islands year-round, but southern populations move north in winter. Lays 2 eggs (rarely 1), but seldom raises 2 chicks. Breeding success generally lower at northern sites, but they are more likely to re-lay following breeding failure at these locations thanks to the longer breeding season. Diet varies among colonies; mainly crustaceans and fish. Most prey species at the Prince Edward Islands are benthic; recently observed attempting to steal large squid prey from conspecifics in the Falklands/Malvinas, which is home to the largest Gentoo population. Dives to 212m (11 minutes), although most dives are shallower, depending on water depth. Witoorpikkewyn

Ad showing orange wash to under-flippers

Displaying ads

Juv showing pale throat and reduced 'ear' patch

The orange bill and feet are prominent at sea

Chinstrap Penguin *Pygoscelis antarcticus* 68–74cm; 3.5–5.2kg

A fairly large penguin with a distinctive, thin black line across its throat and face. Told from Adelie Penguin by white face with striking dark eyes. Juv has speckled grey face. Island, but not recorded from sthn Africa. Lays 1 or 2 eggs. Eats mainly crustaceans, especially Antarctic krill; dives to 180m (5 minutes), but most dives <40m. **Bandkeelpikkewyn**

Voice: Display call '*ah kawk kawk kawk*'; usually silent at sea. **Status and biology:** 7 million pairs breed on Antarctic Peninsula and surrounding islands in summer, including Bouvet. Closely associated with sea ice; numbers decreasing in north of range. Occasional vagrants reach Marion

Ad showing striking face pattern

Ad porpoising

Ad in colony, with soiled belly plumage

Chinstrap Penguins often occur in flocks at sea or on ice floes

Adelie Penguin *Pygoscelis adeliae*

70–72cm; 3.8–6.6kg

A fairly large penguin with broad white eye-rings. Feathers on rear of crown can be raised into a short crest. Feathers extend over base of bill. Juv has white throat, but face black (unlike Chinstrap Penguin). **Voice:** Trumpeting display call '*arr-ar-ar-ar-ar-raaa*'; usually silent at sea. **Status and biology:** Not threatened globally despite the impacts of climate change on populations at northern breeding sites, where reduction in sea ice are driving population decreases; increasing locally in south of its range. 2.4 million pairs breed at ice-free areas in Antarctica and surrounding islands in summer, including a few on Bouvet. Typically remains near sea ice; occasional vagrants reach Marion Island, but not recorded from sthn Africa. Lays 1 or 2 eggs.

Eats mainly crustaceans, especially Antarctic krill; dives to 180m (6 minutes), but most dives <20m. Adeliepikkewyn

Ads porpoising

Ad showing short bill with feathered base

Adelie Penguins are curious birds, often walking up to investigate people

King Penguin *Aptenodytes patagonicus* 88–95cm; 9–15kg

A large, long-flippered penguin with distinctive orange neck patches and pinkish-orange or lavender plates on the sides of its bill. Smaller and more slender than Emperor Penguin, with a longer bill and neater, richer coloration. Juv duller with creamy neck patches. **Voice:** Loud, trumpeted '*dhu-du-du-du*' at colonies; occasional '*dhuu*' at sea. **Status and biology:** 2.2 million pairs worldwide; 225,000 pairs at the Prince Edward Islands where numbers are decreasing, and listed as **NEAR THREATENED** in South Africa. Common at sub-Antarctic islands, but forages mainly in Antarctic waters. Very rare vagrant to South Africa. Clumsy ashore; breeds year-round in dense colonies on flat ground with sheltered landing beaches. Lays

1 egg; incubated by both sexes on their feet; few chicks hatched in late summer survive. Eats mainly myctophid fish, also some squid and crustaceans; dives bimodal, 10–40m and 140–330m (max 343m, 9 minutes). Koningpikkewyn

Juvs are duller and mostly remain at sea

Ads carry the egg or small chick on their feet

Ads are easily identified at sea by their extensive orange ear patches and long bill stripe

Emperor Penguin *Aptenodytes forsteri*

100–130cm; 20–38kg

The largest penguin; confined mainly to Antarctic pack ice, although a few juvs stray north to peri-Antarctic islands. Much larger than King Penguin, with proportionately shorter bill and flippers; neck patches less well defined and mainly golden (not orange); bill stripe smaller. Imm paler with whitish neck patches and dull bill stripe; juv has dark eye patches in whitish face. At sea, appears bulkier than King Penguin, with a shorter neck; body rides higher in the water. **Voice:** Loud, trumpeted '*hra-ra-ra-ra*' at colonies; usually silent at sea. **Status and biology: NEAR THREATENED.** 238,000 pairs breed on fast ice around Antarctica in winter. Not recorded in sthn Africa; fairly common in areas with sea ice. Males huddle together to incubate the single egg on their feet, losing 40% of mass during 3–4-month fast; feed chicks an oil-rich oesophageal secretion until females return. Eats fish, squid and crustaceans; dives to 564m (22 minutes). Keiserpikkewyn

Recently fledged juvs at sea

Ads are normally seen resting on ice floes

Emperor Penguins are larger than King Penguins, with shorter bill and small orange neck patch

A male Wandering Albatross displays to a young female on Marion Island

ALBATROSSES

Albatrosses (Diomedeidae) are large, long-winged seabirds that are the largest of the tubenoses (Procellariiformes), although the smallest albatrosses weigh barely half as much as the giant petrels. The taxonomy of some species complexes remains debated, but generally 21 species in 4 genera are recognised, 17 in the southern hemisphere, 1 in the tropical Pacific and 3 in the North Pacific. Although currently no albatrosses breed in the North Atlantic, recent fossil remains have been found on Bermuda.

Albatrosses are premier exponents of dynamic soaring, which exploits differences in wind speed between wave troughs and peaks to generate lift. This allows these birds to cover vast distances with little energy expenditure unless they are forced to fly directly into the wind. Heart rate monitors show that under most conditions, the heart rates of flying albatrosses are similar to those of birds resting on land. However, taking off requires more effort, especially in relatively calm conditions, as does flying into strong headwinds. Their long wings make them rather

buoyant, so most species seldom dive more than a metre or two below the surface.

The sexes usually look alike, but males average slightly larger, especially in bill depth. Juveniles have distinct plumages in most species, taking several years to acquire adult plumage. In the Wandering Albatross complex, plumage becomes gradually whiter with age, progressing faster in males than females. Albatrosses are so large that they seldom moult all their flight feathers each year unless they take a year off between breeding attempts. Immatures usually alternate replacing the 3 outer or 7 inner primaries each year, although with some individual variation. Some juvenile coverts may be retained for up to 4 years. Most species do not overlap moult with breeding, but the Falklands/ Malvinas population of Black-browed Albatrosses starts moult while still feeding chicks.

All albatrosses are socially monogamous and usually keep the same mate for as long as both partners are alive, but 5–15% of chicks result from extra-pair fertilisations. They lay a single, white egg, usually on a nest mound. The few instances of 2-egg clutches result from 2 females laying in the same nest. They do not re-lay if the first egg is lost. The sexes share incubation duties. Albatross chicks are semi-altricial, and are fed by regurgitation by both parents, who alternate staying with the chick for the first few weeks during the brood-guard phase. After breeding, adults disperse widely. Among many species, the breeding cycle is so protracted that they usually take a year off after a successful breeding attempt.

Juvenile albatrosses receive no assistance from their parents after they leave their breeding islands, which is incongruous, given the time and effort invested in raising them to the point of fledging. Juveniles tend to drift downwind from their colonies, gradually travelling farther

and farther each day as they learn their craft – or they fail to improve their flight skills and die. Only about half of all fledglings return to their breeding islands after 3–7 years.

Of the 22 species recognised by the IUCN, 15 are globally threatened and 6 are Near Threatened, making albatrosses among the most threatened family of birds. The main threat to most species is accidental bycatch on fishing gear, but they are also affected by pollution (especially plastic litter in the North Pacific) and disturbance of their breeding islands, including the introduction of mammal predators. Mice are significant predators of albatross chicks at both Marion and Gough islands. Eradicating mice from these islands is a key conservation priority.

Grey-headed and Indian Yellow-nosed albatrosses breed together on the northern cliffs of Prince Edward Island

GREAT ALBATROSSES *DIOMEDEA*

The largest albatrosses; all species have pink bills and mostly white underwings at all ages. Previously only 2 species – Royal and Wandering albatrosses – were recognised; recent splits have greatly complicated the identification of the 6 species, at least 5 of which occur off sthn Africa. A few individuals from the 2 New Zealand populations (*D. a. antipodensis* and *D. a. gibsoni*) might be overlooked in the region.

Northern Royal Albatross *Diomedea sanfordi*   107–122cm; 6–8kg

Similar size and shape as Wandering Albatross (p.44), but head looks sleeker due to shallower forehead; bill yellow-pink with a black cutting edge visible at close range. Usually lacks pink mark on neck typical of Wandering Albatross complex. Best identified by crisp black upperwing contrasting with white body and tail. Underwing is like that of Wandering Albatross, but has broader black carpal patch. Juv has some black in outer tail and slight scalloping on back, but has much less black in tail than a Wandering Albatross, with dark upperwings. Black carpal patch narrower than in ad. **Voice:** Silent at sea.

Status and biology: ENDANGERED. 5,800 pairs breed in New Zealand each year, almost all on the Chatham Islands. Main threats include long-line fishing and climate change, with extreme storms stripping soil from breeding sites, greatly reducing breeding success. Br ads forage in New Zealand waters; imms and non-br ads disperse across the S Pacific to the Patagonian Shelf, with many continuing eastward past Africa to reach New Zealand. Rare visitor to South Africa, mainly along the shelf edge. Attends fishing vessels more than Wandering Albatross. Eats mainly squid.
Swartvlerkkoningalbatros

Juv taking off, showing black leading edges to wings

Juv showing black upperwings, mottled back and tail tip

Ad showing black carpal marks

JOHN GRAHAM

Southern Royal Albatross *Diomedea epomophora* 115–122cm; 7–11kg

Similar to Northern Royal Albatross, but upperwing whitens with age from leading edge; carpal bar narrower at least in adults. Juv is similar to juv Northern Royal Albatross; may retain mainly black upperwing and some black in outer tail and on scapulars for 10–12 years. White tail separates it from Wandering Albatross (p.44), except for very old birds. Upperwing generally more finely marked than equivalent Wandering Albatross, and usually lacks pink mark on neck; head looks sleeker due to shallower forehead; bill yellow-pink with a black cutting edge visible at close range. **Voice:** Silent at sea.

Status and biology: VULNERABLE. 7,900 pairs breed at islands off New Zealand each year, almost all on Campbell Island. The population has been increasing steadily for the last 60 years following the cessation of farming and removal of introduced mammals from Campbell. Br ads forage in New Zealand waters; imms and non-br ads disperse across the S Pacific to sthn S America, returning via the Pacific. Rare visitor to South Africa. Became a regular visitor off Africa in the 1990s and early 2000s, possibly linked to fishing for Patagonian toothfish around the Prince Edward Islands. At this time it was more common in oceanic waters than Northern Royal Albatross. Eats mainly squid. **Witvlerkkoningalbatros**

Ad showing reduced black carpal mark

Ad on the water; note black cutting edge to bill

Ad with finely marked upperwing

Juv with mostly black upperwing

Juv from below

43

Wandering Albatross *Diomedea exulans* 110–135cm; 6.8–10kg

A huge, hump-backed albatross with a pink bill. Underwing white with black tip, trailing edge and leading edge to carpal joint. Juv chocolate-brown, with white face and underwings. As birds age, they become progressively whiter: body becomes mottled ('leopard' stage), then all-white, with fine vermiculations concentrated on back and breast, forming shadow breast band; then upperwing starts to whiten, initially from centre of wing over elbow (not from leading edge, as in Southern Royal Albatross, p.43). Throughout these stages, birds have a black tail tip (mostly white in royal albatrosses). Males whiten faster than females; after 20 years, black only on flight feathers and a few covert tips. Old

Male Wandering Albatross on nest with female adjacent

Old male from above

Male/old female from above

Ad from below

males differ from ad Southern Royal Albatross in pinker bill with no dark cutting edge. Feathering does not extend far onto lower mandible (as is the case in royal albatrosses), giving a steeper-looking forehead. Often has pink mark on side of neck (rare in royal albatrosses). Very hard to separate from Tristan Albatross (p.46). **Voice:** Grunts, whinnies and rapidly vibrates bill in display; occasionally calls and displays at sea. **Status and biology: VULNERABLE.** 8,000 pairs breed at sub-Antarctic islands each year; 3,600 pairs at Prince Edward Islands. Regular in oceanic waters off sthn Africa; occasionally visits trawlers, but seldom joins feeding mêlée. Lays 1 egg in summer; takes 11 months from laying to fledging; rarely breeds in year following a successful attempt. Non-br ads mostly remain in the S Indian and E Atlantic oceans, but a few birds circle the Southern Ocean. Eats mainly squid and carrion. Grootalbatros

Juv displaying to imm male at sea

Juv upperparts

Juv underparts

Ad female/young male from above

Young female/imm male from above

Imm from below

Tristan Albatross *Diomedea dabbenena* 100–110cm; 5–8kg

Slightly smaller than Wandering Albatross (p.44), with a shorter bill; plumage takes longer to whiten, never attaining fully white plumage of old male Wandering Albatrosses, but some old males have mostly white upperwing coverts. Most birds at sea probably not identifiable with certainty; ad males typically have a mostly dark upperwing with a pale elbow patch but less black in tail tip than Wandering Albatrosses at similar upperwing stage; they apparently never show any vermiculations in the tail feathers. Some ad females retain brown feathers on the crown, back, breast and flanks, but old females resemble ad males. Some juvs and imms have a blackish cutting edge to the upper mandible

Male Tristan Albatross on nest with female alongside

Old ad male from above   Typical ad male from above   Old female or young ad male

and a dusky bill tip, similar to Amsterdam Albatross (p.48). **Voice:** Similar to that of Wandering Albatross. In full display, spreads wings and throws head back. **Status and biology:** CRITICALLY ENDANGERED. 2,200 pairs breed each year, almost all on Gough Island; only 1 or 2 pairs on Inaccessible Island, Tristan da Cunha. Remains mainly in the S Atlantic but some non-br birds and juvs disperse into the Indian Ocean, reaching Australia. Abundance off sthn Africa poorly known due to difficulty of identifying birds at sea. Br ads forage in a broad area from 28–48°S, between 50°W and 10°E. Many non-br ads forage in oceanic waters SW of Africa, with a secondary 'hotspot' off N Namibia. Favours fairly warm water (15–20°C), >1,000m deep. Breeding biology is similar to that of Wandering Albatross, but suffers high chick mortality due to mouse predation at Gough Island. Eats mainly squid and carrion.

Tristangrootalbatros

Imm male and female on Gough Island

Unusually white male from above

15-year old female

Imm female from above

Imm with dark cutting edge to bill

Amsterdam Albatross *Diomedea amsterdamensis* 100–110cm; 6–7kg

Slightly smaller than Wandering Albatross (p.44), with a shorter bill; structure similar to Tristan Albatross (p.46). Bill has a dusky tip and dark cutting edge to upper mandible like that of royal albatrosses (pp.42–43), but these features also shown by some young Tristan Albatrosses. Birds at sea probably not identifiable with certainty unless white plastic ring seen (almost the entire population is colour-ringed). Breeds in dark-backed plumage, similar to juv or early imm Wandering Albatross plumage. **Voice:** Similar to that of Wandering Albatross. **Status and biology: ENDANGERED.** 30–40 pairs breed each year at Amsterdam Island, central Indian Ocean; total population <500 birds. Threats include long-line fishing mortality, introduced predators and diseases that increase chick mortality. Disperses across S Indian Ocean, occasionally reaching oceanic waters off east coast of South Africa. **Amsterdamgrootalbatros**

Ad female from below   Ad female showing black cutting edge to bill

Ad male off Amsterdam Island   Ad male from below   Ad female from above

MOLLYMAWKS

Medium-sized to small, dark-backed albatrosses confined to the Southern Ocean. Each species has diagnostic bill and underwing patterns, although bill colour changes and underwing whitens with age in some species. Identification of juveniles and immatures in the Shy Albatross complex is not well understood; probably only adults and sub-adults can be separated reliably at sea.

A vagrant Buller's Albatross (right) confronts Indian (front) and Atlantic (back) yellow-nosed albatrosses

Buller's Albatross *Thalassarche bulleri*

76–81cm; 2.2–3.3kg

A fairly small mollymawk with neat underwing at all ages; pattern similar to that of yellow-nosed albatrosses (pp.50–51), but margins fractionally narrower. Head and neck washed grey, with pale forecrown. Ad's bill has broad yellow stripe along upper mandible and narrow stripe on lower mandible. 2 subspecies sometimes split: 'Pacific Albatross' *T. b. platei* has a darker grey head than *T. b. bulleri*, with pale crown restricted to front half of the head, not extending onto the hind-crown as in nominate. Ad most likely confused with ad Atlantic Yellow-nosed (p.50) or Grey-headed (p.52) albatrosses. Juv has dark horn-coloured bill with black tip and smooth grey wash on head and neck; could be confused with juv Shy Albatross (p.53). **Voice:** Silent at sea. **Status and biology:** NEAR THREATENED.

30,000 pairs breed at islands off New Zealand; 13,500 pairs of *T. b. bulleri* at the Snares and Solander islands, and 16,500 pairs of *T. b. platei* at the Chatham and Three Kings islands. Forages mainly between Australia and the west coast of S America, with most non-br birds feeding in the Humboldt Current. Rare vagrant to South Africa; most records are of birds attending trawlers along the shelf edge from Cape Town to Mossel Bay. Eats fish and squid. Witkroonalbatros

Juv taking off showing head similar to juv Shy Albatross but broader black underwing margins

Ad showing neat, narrow underwing margins

Ad on the water

Atlantic Yellow-nosed Albatross *Thalassarche chlororhynchos* 72–80cm; 1.8–2.8kg

A small, slender albatross with a relatively long bill. Underwing has crisp black margin, with leading edge roughly twice as broad as trailing edge. Ad has black bill with yellow stripe along upper mandible, becoming reddish towards tip. Differs from Indian Yellow-nosed Albatross in having grey wash on head and nape (slightly paler on forecrown) and extensive, dark grey feathers around eyes; at close range, base of yellow stripe on upper mandible is broad and rounded (not pointed). Juv bill mostly black; head white; similar to juv Indian Yellow-nosed Albatross, but tends to show more extensive dark eye patch and grey wash on mantle. In the hand, shape of plates at base of bill differs. Bill starts to develop yellow culminicorn during first year. **Voice:** High-pitched reeling call in flight and on ground at colonies, given with head thrown back and yellow gape stripes exposed; throaty '*waah*' and '*weeeeh*' notes when squabbling over food. **Status and biology:** ENDANGERED; exploitation at Tristan colonies drove rapid population decreases prior to the species' protection in 1976; population largely stable over last few decades despite some mortality in long-line fisheries. 32,000 pairs breed in sparse colonies in summer, usually on level ground at Tristan da Cunha and Gough Island. Fairly common year-round in small numbers mainly off the west coast of sthn Africa; often the most abundant albatross off Namibia. During incubation, ads forage mainly along the shelf edge from sthn Angola to Cape Agulhas. Rare in SW Indian Ocean. Eats fish, squid and crustaceans. Atlantiese Geelneusalbatros

Ad shows yellow gape when aroused

Juv prior to fledging

Ad from above

Ad from below

Imm from above

Indian Yellow-nosed Albatross *Thalassarche carteri* 75–80cm; 1.9–2.7kg

Slightly larger than Atlantic Yellow-nosed Albatross; head appears smaller. Ad has only a faint grey wash on the cheek and less extensive dark feathering around eyes, giving it a more open face; at close range, base of yellow bill stripe is pointed (not rounded). Juv similar to juv Atlantic Yellow-nosed Albatross, but has smaller dark eye patch and less extensive grey wash on mantle. **Voice:** Similar to that of Atlantic Yellow-nosed Albatross. **Status and biology: ENDANGERED.** 41,500 pairs breed in dense, cliff-side colonies at S Indian Ocean islands in summer (not in sparse colonies on level ground as do Atlantic Yellow-nosed Albatrosses). Amsterdam Island has the largest population, but numbers decreasing here mainly due to avian cholera. Also fairly often caught on long-lines, but this does not cause decreases in other populations; the 7,000 pairs breeding at Prince Edward Island appear to be stable or slowly increasing, but recent counts are needed (does not breed on Marion Island). Fairly common off sthn Africa year-round; ventures farther north in winter. It is the most common albatross off KZN, and often off the E Cape. Mostly found in the Indian Ocean, but some range into the SE Atlantic Ocean, occasionally reaching Tristan and Gough, even coming ashore in Atlantic Yellow-nosed Albatross colonies. Confiding; frequently visits fishing vessels, and uses its aerial agility to snatch scraps ahead of larger albatrosses. Eats fish, squid and crustaceans as well as fishery discards. Indiese Geelneusalbatros

Ad on the water

Juv on the water

Ad from above

Ad from below

Imm from below

Grey-headed Albatross *Thalassarche chrysostoma* 75–88cm; 2.6–4.2kg

Similar to Black-browed Albatross, showing comparable progression of underwing coloration with age. Ad has grey head, paler grey neck and black bill with yellow stripe along upper and lower mandibles. Juv has darker grey head (although cheeks almost white in some individuals), merging into mantle, giving a more bull-necked appearance. Juv bill all-dark (not black-tipped); soon develops yellow tinge to central ridge of upper mandible. **Voice:** Rattling display call at colonies; squawks when squabbling over food. **Status and biology:** ENDANGERED. 95,000 pairs breed at sub-Antarctic islands each year; 9,500 pairs at the Prince Edward Islands. Population decreasing, mainly due to decreases at South Georgia and Campbell Island. Population stable at Marion Island, despite many ads (mostly males) killed by toothfish long-lining in the 1990s; chicks killed by introduced mice in recent years. Breeds in summer, but chicks fledge only in May so most pairs take a year off after raising a chick. Non-breeders disperse widely throughout the Southern Ocean, with many individuals circling Antarctica. Rare visitor to sthn Africa, mostly juv birds, Jun–Sept; joins other albatrosses feeding at trawlers. Ads largely remain south of the Subtropical Convergence. Eats mainly squid. **Gryskopalbatros**

Juv sitting on the water

Ad from above; juv showing grey-washed 'bull-neck' (inset)

Ad from below; juv from below (inset)

Shy Albatross *Thalassarche cauta*

90–100cm; 3.0–5.2kg

Largest mollymawk, with extensive white on underwing; upperwing and mantle paler than in other mollymawks; very rarely has white back. Underwing has narrow black border; black 'thumb-print' on leading edge near body diagnostic for the Shy Albatross complex (including vagrant Salvin's and Chatham albatrosses, pp.54 55). Ad has pale grey cheeks and white crown; bill pale olive-grey with yellow tip. Imm has grey-washed head, often with incomplete grey breast band; bill is grey with black tip. Fresh juv has smooth grey wash on head and neck, recalling Salvin's Albatross. Often treated as 2 species: Shy Albatross (*T. c. cauta*) averages slightly smaller than White-capped Albatross (*T. c. steadi*) and most ads have a yellow base to the culminicorn. Genetic evidence shows that only 5% of birds caught on longlines off sthn Africa are *T. c. cauta*, all of which are juvs or imms that are not separable from *T. c. steadi*. **Voice:** Loud, raucous '*waak*' when squabbling over food. **Status and biology:** NEAR THREATENED. 100,000 pairs of *T. c. steadi* breed at islands off New Zealand each year and 15,000 pairs of *T. c. cauta* off Tasmania; one pair of *T. c. steadi* bred on Prince Edward Island in 2008. Most *T. c. steadi* that breed successfully probably skip the following year, whereas most *T. c. cauta* breed annually. Common non-br visitor to fishing grounds along shelf edge; generally occurs closer to land than other albatrosses; uncommon in oceanic waters. Eats mainly fish; also squid, crustaceans, tunicates and fishery wastes. **Bloubekalbatros**

Imm on the water

Ad and imm (inset) from above

Sub-ad from below showing 'thumb-print'

Salvin's Albatross *Thalassarche salvini*

90–100cm; 3.3–4.9kg

Forms part of the Shy Albatross complex; underwing similar at all ages. Ad has grey wash to neck and face, contrasting with pale crown; bill grey-sided with paler, yellowish band along upper and lower mandible, and dark spot on lower mandible tip. Imm is similar to imm Shy Albatross (p.53), but with darker underwing (broader carpal patch and fully black primary feathers); head averages darker grey and often shows dark back extending onto rump. **Voice:** Silent at sea. **Status and biology: VULNERABLE.** 32,000 pairs breed off New Zealand (Bounties and Snares islands); at least 5 pairs breed among other mollymawks at two islands in W Crozets, where seemingly increasing. Occasional vagrant ashore on Gough Island. Most birds remain in the Pacific Ocean, wintering mainly off the west coast of S America. Rare vagrant to the shelf edge off the W Cape and in the Southern Ocean. Eats squid and fishery wastes. Salvinalbatros

Ad on the water

Imm on the water

Juv showing paler crown

Juv (left) with imm Buller's Albatross off Chile

Ad from below

Ad from above

Imm from below

Imm from above

Chatham Albatross *Thalassarche eremita*

90–100cm; 3.1–4.7kg

Forms part of the Shy Albatross complex; underwing similar at all ages. Ad has unmistakable yellow bill with dark tip to lower mandible, and dark, uniform grey head. Juv similar to juv Salvin's Albatross, but averages even darker on head and neck and has a dusky yellow bill with a dark tip. **Voice:** Silent at sea. **Status and biology:** VULNERABLE. 4,500 pairs breed on Pyramid Rock, Chatham Islands, New Zealand; population stable. Most birds remain in the Pacific Ocean, wintering mainly off the west coast of S America. Rare vagrant; only a handful of records all attending fishing vessels at the W Cape shelf edge in winter. Eats squid and fishery wastes. Chathamalbatros

Ad on the water

Ad taking off

Juv has darker head than juv Salvin's Albatross

Ad from below

Ad from above

55

Black-browed Albatross *Thalassarche melanophris* 80–95cm; 2.2–4.2kg

Medium-sized mollymawk. Ad has an orange bill with a reddish tip, and a small black eyebrow. Ad underwing has a broad black leading edge and narrower trailing edge, only slightly less extensive than that of Campbell Albatross. Juv underwing dark grey with a paler centre, lightening with age. Juv bill dark horn-grey with a black tip, gradually becoming yellow with a darker tip. Amount of grey on head and neck is variable, usually forming incomplete collar. **Voice:** Grunts and squawks when squabbling over food. **Status and biology:** Not threatened globally thanks to ongoing increases at the Falklands/Malvinas and islands off Chile, but listed as **ENDANGERED** in Namibia and South Africa, where most birds come from the declining population on South Georgia. 700,000 pairs breed at sub-Antarctic islands (200,000 pairs) and Falklands/Malvinas (500,000 pairs) in summer; one mated with a Grey-headed Albatross at Marion Island in some years. Common year-round off sthn Africa; ads mostly present Apr–Sept. Juvs rapidly disperse east after fledging, arriving off the Cape within 3–4 weeks of leaving South Georgia, while still growing their outer primaries. Most abundant at shelf edge associated with fishing vessels, but also in oceanic waters; usually close inshore only during storms. Eats squid, fish, crustaceans and fishery wastes. Br ads tend to forage repeatedly in the same areas, but this is more marked in males and younger ads. Swartrugalbatros

Ad (top) and imm (above) on water

Ad from below

Ad from above

Imm from above; juv from below (inset)

Campbell Albatross *Thalassarche impavida*   80–95cm; 2.2–4.2kg

Very similar to Black-browed Albatross; ad distinguished by pale, honey-coloured eyes and slightly more extensive black margins to the underwing; often appears more slender. Juv and young imm probably not separable from juv and imm Black-browed Albatross; pale eyes start to be distinctive from 2–3 years old. **Voice:** Grunts and squawks when squabbling over food. **Status and biology:** VULNERABLE; population decreased rapidly during the 1970s and 1980s due to bycatch on longlines but has been slowly recovering for the last few decades. 21,000 pairs breed at Campbell Island, south of New Zealand, in summer. Most winter from the SE Indian Ocean across the S Pacific to Chile; only known south of Africa from one adult that was tracked circumnavigating the Southern Ocean. Ranges of juv and imm poorly known due to difficulty separating from Black-browed Albatross. Ads are more oceanic than Black-browed Albatross, and often venture south to the edge of the Antarctic pack ice in summer, but in winter they range farther north, usually in water >15°C. Eats squid, fish, crustaceans and fishery wastes. Campbellalbatros

Ad (top) and imm (above) on water

Ad from above

Imm from below   Juv from below

Sooty Albatross *Phoebetria fusca*

84–90cm; 2.1–3.2kg

The two *Phoebetria* albatrosses have sooty brown plumage, white eye-rings, long, wedge-shaped tails, and exceptionally long and narrow wings; appear more slender than giant petrels (pp.64–65); dynamic soaring flight is very different from flap-and-glide flight of juv gannets (pp.132–133). Ad Sooty Albatross is readily identified by its dark brown plumage, with pale shafts to primary and tail feathers. At close range, yellow stripe is visible on lower mandible (all-black in juvs). Juvs and imms show a variable pale collar and mottling on back, but this does not extend to rump as in Light-mantled Albatross. **Voice:** Wailing '*peeoooo*' call in flight and from cliffs at colonies; silent at sea. **Status and biology:** ENDANGERED. 13,500 pairs breed at sub-Antarctic islands each year, including 7,500 pairs at Tristan da Cunha/Gough Island and 3,300 pairs at the Prince Edward Islands, where numbers are increasing, although chicks have been killed by mice in recent years. Fairly common south of 38°S; uncommon visitor to oceanic waters off sthn Africa year-round; vagrant to shelf waters. Breeds on cliffs in summer; chicks fledge only in May so rarely breeds in year following a successful attempt. Eats mainly squid; also prions and other small seabirds. **Bruinalbatros**

Ad at nest site on Gough Island

Ad from above

Ad from below

Imm showing pale neck

Light-mantled Albatross *Phoebetria palpebrata*   80–90cm; 2.2–3.2kg

Slightly larger than Sooty Albatross; ad has a much paler, greyish back that contrasts with the head and upperwings. At close range, the incomplete white eye-ring is shorter and broader, and lower mandible has a lilac (not yellow) stripe. On land, head appears peaked (rounded in Sooty Albatross). Juvs average slightly paler above than juv Sooty Albatrosses; best identified by their eye-ring which is shorter, broader and paler than that of juv Sooty Albatrosses. Imms have mottled body, with pale plumage extending onto lower back (not confined to neck) and appear colder grey-brown than imm Sooty Albatrosses. **Voice:** Wailing cry similar to that of Sooty Albatross; silent at sea. **Status and biology:** NEAR THREATENED. 20,000 pairs breed at sub-Antarctic and peri-Antarctic islands each year;

350 pairs at the Prince Edward Islands, where numbers are decreasing. Typically forages farther south than Sooty Albatross; fairly common south of the Antarctic Convergence; regular to Subtropical Convergence but a rare vagrant to sthn African waters, mainly off the east coast, where occasional birds wander far north in winter, sometimes reaching tropical waters. Breeding biology and diet similar to that of Sooty Albatross, but lays 3–4 weeks later. Swartkopalbatros

Ad at nest site on Prince Edward Island

Ad from above

Ad from below

Imm showing pale, mottled head and back

Laysan Albatross *Phoebastria immutabilis* 80cm; 2.6–4.0kg

A small, slender albatross, superficially similar to an imm Black-browed Albatross (p.56), but with dark-washed cheek, brown lower back extending onto rump, and distinctive underwing pattern with black streaks on underwing coverts; pinkish feet project beyond tail in flight. Juv resembles ad; bill slightly greyer. **Voice:** Silent at sea. **Status and biology: NEAR THREATENED.** 590,000 pairs breed at islands in the N Pacific; very rare vagrant in southern hemisphere; only 2 records from SW Indian Ocean, both in the 1980s and possibly referring to the same individual. Eats squid and fish. Swartwangalbatros

Ad on the water showing dusky face

Dark back extends onto rump

Taking off

Underwing pattern is diagnostic

Moulting primaries

A pair of Southern Giant Petrels at their northernmost breeding site on Gough Island

PETRELS, PRIONS AND SHEARWATERS

Comprising some 96 species in 16 genera, the petrels (Procellariidae) are the second-largest family of seabirds, after the gulls, terns and skimmers. They occur worldwide and range in size from the tiny Bulwer's Petrel (100g) to the giant petrels (up to 5.5kg). Given the large number of species, it is not surprising that the family is diverse. Major groupings include the giant petrels (*Macronectes*) and other fulmarine petrels (*Fulmarus, Daption, Thalassoica, Pagodroma*), the prions (*Pachyptila*) and closely-related Blue (*Halobaena*) and Kerguelen Petrels (*Aphrodroma*),

Grey Petrel breeding in a cave on Marion Island

the speciose gadfly petrels (*Pterodroma*), and a large group of other petrels (*Procellaria, Bulweria, Pseudobulweria*) and shearwaters (*Calonectris, Ardenna, Puffinus*). The diving petrels (*Pelecanoides*) used to be placed in their own family, but genetic data indicate that they are nested within the petrels. However, their closest relatives within the petrels remain disputed.

Given the large diversity within the family, petrels occupy a range of niches. Like albatrosses, most species use dynamic soaring to travel large distances at low cost. However, flight efficiency is traded off against diving ability, with a continuum from the highly aerial gadfly petrels, through the shearwaters to the specialist diving petrels that struggle to stay aloft even while flapping frantically; soaring is out of the question. Even within the shearwaters, wing loading increases from aerial, mainly warm-water species such as the Wedge-tailed and *Calonectris* shearwaters, through more generalist species such as Great and Flesh-footed shearwaters, to proficient divers such as Sooty and *Puffinus* shearwaters. Gait on land is clumsy and, apart from giant petrels, they seldom come ashore except when breeding (although some species return to their breeding

61

Great Shearwaters arrive at dusk off Richmond Hill, Gough Island

burrows after moulting – quite why they do so is unclear, especially as they often suffer predation by skuas at this time).

The sexes look alike, but males average larger, especially in giant petrels and the Snow Petrel. Juveniles lack distinct plumages in most species; only the two giant petrels show complex age-related variation in plumage. Several gadfly petrels and a few fulmarine petrels and shearwaters have two or more colour morphs. All species replace all primaries each year, but this is a struggle for the giant petrels, which are the largest birds to do so without becoming flightless. Giant petrels start to moult while breeding (especially the larger males), as do several other petrels, but most species delay until the chicks are ready to fledge. Moulting can be intense, with up to 7 primaries replaced at once. This has a large impact on wing area, and petrels often spend a greater proportion of the day sitting

on the water while moulting than at other times of the year. Among diving petrels, some birds may entirely lose the ability to fly while moulting. The greater secondary coverts are moulted with the inner primaries, and usually are fully grown before secondary moult commences, which allows large numbers of secondaries to be replaced at once without greatly decreasing the wing area. However, most species of fulmarine and *Procellaria* petrels, as well as some gadfly petrels and a few *Ardenna* shearwaters, don't replace all their secondaries each year.

Breeding biology is similar to that of the albatrosses; all are monogamous, lay a single, white egg, and the parents share incubation and chick-rearing duties. They do not re-lay if the first egg is lost. Most species breed in burrows or rock crevices, and many are nocturnal at their breeding sites, thus reducing the risk of predation

Petrel chicks have a thick layer of down (Broad-billed Prion, left), which they shed just before fledging (Great Shearwater, right)

by skuas or other predatory birds. Adults cease feeding their chicks even before they fledge, and give them no assistance thereafter. Adults disperse widely after breeding, with some species making trans-equatorial migrations to take advantage of seasonally abundant resources in both hemispheres.

At least 2 species have gone extinct since 1500; of the 96 extant species, 43 are globally threatened and 11 are Near Threatened. Some genera have higher proportions of Threatened species than others (e.g. 4 of 5 *Procellaria*, 3 of 4 *Pseudobulweria* and 23 of 34 *Pterodroma* petrels are Threatened). The main threat to most species is the introduction of mammal predators

to their breeding islands, such as House Mice on Gough and Marion islands. Some 2,000 feral cats on Marion Island killed an estimated 450,000 seabirds, mainly petrels, each year, before they were eradicated in 1991. Petrels are also prone to disturbance of their breeding islands, including the impact of light pollution, which disorients birds commuting to and from their colonies at night. Fledglings leaving the island for the first time are particularly susceptible, often crashing into buildings or streetlights. Some species, notably *Procellaria* petrels and large shearwaters, are caught on fishing gear, and many species accumulate large amounts of ingested plastic.

Dealing with the doldrums

Albatrosses are widely regarded as great ocean wanderers, but they are largely confined to higher latitudes where reliable winds assist their dynamic soaring flight. They mostly avoid the tropics, where the infamous doldrums make life miserable for sailors – and seabirds – that rely on the wind for propulsion. However, several shearwaters routinely cross the tropics to exploit the seasonal flush of production in both the northern and southern hemispheres. These include three of the most abundant seabirds in the world: Short-tailed, Sooty and Great shearwaters.

Like albatrosses and other petrels, these long-distance migrants follow routes that limit their energy expenditure by maximising exposure to tailwinds or crosswinds to aid dynamic soaring. However, there are times when the wind dies, or they face headwinds that force them to spend more energy on flapping. Recent tracking studies allow us to match a bird's position to the local winds, to infer how often this occurs, and where it is likely to be a challenge. As expected, Great Shearwaters returning to their breeding islands in the central South Atlantic face the most adversity in crossing the Equator. By going east before heading south, they ensure favourable winds in the North Atlantic.

Great Shearwater gliding in near-calm conditions

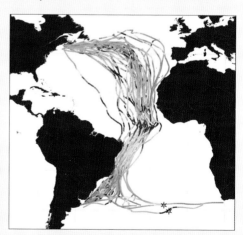

Tracks of Great Shearwaters returning to their breeding islands (stars) from their wintering area in the NW Atlantic. Green sections indicate favourable winds; red sections adverse wind conditions (from Powers *et al.* 2022, *Frontiers in Marine Science* doi: 10.3389/fmars.2022.938033)

Northern Giant Petrel *Macronectes halli* 81–98cm; 3.1–5.8kg

Giant petrels are the largest petrels – huge, lumbering birds weighing more than small albatrosses, with massive, pale bills. Northern Giant Petrel has a reddish tip to the bill, which appears dark-tipped at a distance. Lacks white morph of Southern Giant Petrel, but old birds can become pale grey. Ad has more uniformly pale grey plumage (not contrasting pale head). Juv is dark brown, becoming paler with age; reddish bill tip is less marked than in ad. **Voice:** Whinnies and neighs in displays and conflicts. **Status and biology:** Not threatened globally, but **NEAR THREATENED** in Namibia and South Africa.

12,000 pairs breed at sub-Antarctic islands; 650 pairs at the Prince Edward Islands. Breeds singly in protected hollows next to rocks, 6 weeks earlier than Southern Giant Petrels. The 2 species are closely related and occasionally hybridise. Fairly common in coastal waters off sthn Africa; scavenges at fishing boats; visits seal colonies more frequently than Southern Giant Petrels. Eats carrion, birds, fish, squid and crustaceans. Smaller females mainly forage at sea, whereas larger males mainly compete at carcasses or hunt birds; kill adult crested penguins at sea and pulls large albatross chicks from their nests. Recently started killing young Wandering Albatross chicks at night in one part of Marion Island. **Grootnellie**

Ad from above; head showing reddish bill tip (inset)

Imm showing mix of paler, worn juv feathers and darker brown imm feathers

Typical ad

Unusually pale ad

Juv on the water showing uniform, fresh plumage

Southern Giant Petrel *Macronectes giganteus* 86–100

Easily confused with Northern Giant Petrel. Ad Southern Giant Petrel typically has a paler head and breast, contrasting with dark body, but definitive identification requires seeing greenish bill tip. Juv is dark brown, very similar to juv Northern Giant Petrel, becoming lighter with age; greenish bill tip not well defined. Rare white morph has odd dark feathers; some leucistic birds are pure white. Size increases farther south; white morph absent from northern colonies. **Voice:** Whinnies and neighs like Northern Giant Petrel. **Status and biology:** Not threatened globally, but NEAR THREATENED in South Africa. 30,000 pairs breed at sub-Antarctic islands; 2,750 pairs breed at the

Prince Edward Islands and 250 pairs at G Island, which is now the northernmost bree site after the population on Tristan da Cunha w hunted to extinction in the 19th century. Breeds in loose colonies in open sites 6 weeks later than Northern Giant Petrel; the 2 species occasionally hybridise. Fairly common in coastal waters around sthn Africa; scavenges at fishing boats and around seal colonies; follows ships in oceanic waters. Diet similar to that of Northern Giant Petrel, but males are less predatory on other birds. Br females spend more time foraging at sea, whereas males remain on the breeding islands, competing for carrion. Males intimidate rivals at carcasses by rushing them with spread wings, raised and fanned tails and erect neck feathers to appear as large and threatening as possible. Reusenellie

Ad showing greenish bill tip

Ad moulting inner primaries

Leucistic bird lacking black spots

Ad from above

Juv in fresh plumage

White morph with some black feathers

m; 2.2–5.8kg
igh
ing
s

...etrel *Daption capense* 35–40cm; 350–550g

, black-and-white ...ith distinctive ...ring on the back, ...ail and upperwing. Tail ...d black. Underparts ...part from black head and wing margins. Very rare leucistic birds may appear all-white, or have only faint greyish markings; could be confused with Snow Petrel (p.69). **Voice:** High-pitched *'cheecheecheechee'* when feeding. **Status and biology:** At least 200,000 pairs breed in summer on Antarctic, peri-Antarctic and sub-Antarctic islands, including hundreds of pairs on Bouvet and the Crozets;

recently a few pairs were found breeding on sea cliffs on the SE coast of Marion Island. Breeds on cliffs or in rock crevices during summer. Common non-br visitor to coastal waters off sthn Africa from May–Nov, with stragglers to Jan. Enthusiastic ship follower, often remaining with a vessel for hours on end. Eats mainly crustaceans when breeding; diet more opportunistic in winter. Gathers in large flocks to scavenge small scraps at fishing boats, often going closer to boats than other scavenging petrels and albatrosses. Particularly favours factory trawlers that process fish on board and discard large volumes of fish scraps. **Seeduifstormvoël**

Cape Petrels are regular ship followers, often approaching closer than other birds, dancing in the ship's updrafts (right)

Cape Petrel taking off

Part of a flock of Cape Petrels feeding with White-chinned Petrels at a trawler

Southern Fulmar *Fulmarus glacialoides*

45–51cm; 680–1,020g

A striking, pale grey petrel with white underparts, whitish tail and white panels in the darker grey outer wing. Dark grey secondaries form a dark trailing edge to the inner wing, contrasting with pale grey coverts. At close range, the dark-tipped, pink bill with blue nostrils is diagnostic. Flight is light and buoyant. **Voice:** High-pitched cackle when squabbling over food. **Status and biology:** Up to 2 million pairs breed in Antarctica and adjacent islands, with the largest populations on South Orkney and South Sandwich islands. Small numbers breed on Bouvet. Breeds in summer, mainly on north-facing cliffs. Rare visitor to sthn Africa, mostly Jun–Oct. Scavenges at trawlers, often among flocks of Cape Petrels. Attracted to ships, and may follow for some time, but less so than Cape Petrel. Numbers reaching the continental shelf vary greatly from year to year; regularly seen on pelagic trips in some years and apparently absent in others. Unusual among petrels in starting to moult its primaries during incubation. Br birds make short foraging trips, lasting only 1–2 days, thus probably obtaining all their food within 400km of their colonies. One colony in E Antarctica collapsed after increased snowfall (linked to climate change) allowed Southern Giant Petrels to access the colony. Eats mainly crustaceans; also fish, squid and fishery wastes. Silwerstormvoël

Southern Fulmars appear dainty sitting on the water

Southern Fulmars are chunky petrels that are easily identified by their pale plumage and striking outer-wing pattern

Antarctic Petrel *Thalassoica antarctica* 40–45cm; 600–780g

A striking brown-and-white petrel with a broad white subterminal band across its wings. Larger than Cape Petrel (p.66); lacks mottled upperparts. Tail is mostly white with a narrow brown tip. Brown upperparts can become quite faded in late summer. **Voice:** Silent at sea. **Status and biology:** At least 500,000 pairs breed at ice-free mountains (nunataks) up to 350km inland in Antarctica and on adjacent islands in the Ross Sea. Largest colony at Swarthamaren, a large nunatak in eastern Dronning Maud Land, S of Africa, where up to 200,000 pairs breed. Common in Antarctic waters, often in large flocks. Occasionally reaches the Prince Edward Islands in winter; very rare vagrant to sthn Africa. Often roosts on icebergs and floes. Eats mainly crustaceans. **Antarktiese Stormvoël**

Antarctic Petrels are easily identified by their striking brown-and-white plumage Moulting birds appear more mottled

Antarctic Petrels are largely confined to areas with sea ice, and often occur in large flocks

Snow Petrel *Pagodroma nivea*

30–40cm; 200–380g

A snow-white petrel with black bill, eyes and feet. Only possible confusion is with a very rare leucistic Cape Petrel (p.66). Largely confined to areas with sea ice, where there is no wave action to allow dynamic soaring. Two races differ in size, probably as a result of historical segregation during past ice ages, but now co-occur and interbreed. **Voice:** Loud screeches at colonies; usually silent at sea. **Status and biology:** At least 65,000 pairs breed in rock crevices at ice-free mountains in Antarctica and adjacent islands in summer, including Bouvet, but population probably much larger. Not recorded from sthn Africa. Eats mainly crustaceans. Witstormvoël

Snow Petrels south of Africa are mainly Lesser Snow Petrels, *P. n. nivea* (left), but larger-billed *P. n. major* also occur (right)

Greater Snow Petrel, *P. n. major*

Snow Petrels moult in late summer

Snow Petrels are not quite as white as the ice floes on which they roost

Blue Petrel *Halobaena caerulea*

28–30cm; 165–250g

A small, blue-grey petrel with white underparts. Superficially similar to prions, but larger, with diagnostic white-tipped tail. Differs from prions in its white frons and black crown and nape, lacking a pale supercilium. At a distance, has darker and better-defined dark grey breast patches, and body is more elongate, tapering from shoulders to relatively long tail. Flight action is more petrel-like – fast and direct, rising higher above water than prions. Juv paler on head; finely scaled white above. **Voice:** Dove-like cooing at breeding islands; silent at sea. **Status and biology:** Not threatened globally, but **NEAR THREATENED** in South Africa. 1 million pairs breed at sub-Antarctic islands in summer, but return to colonies sporadically year-round; 145,000 pairs breed at Marion Island, with probably a similar number at Prince Edward Island; hundreds of pairs recently discovered breeding on Gough Island. Breeds in dense colonies; ads moult shortly after breeding in Mar–Apr, mainly in Antarctic waters SW of Africa, then return to colonies in Apr–May. Rare visitor to sthn Africa; usually remains south of 45°S but occasionally irrupts north in large numbers; in 1984 irruptions occurred to S America and Australasia as well as sthn Africa. Eats mainly crustaceans, but scavenges anything that floats, including insects and bits of plastic. **Bloustormvoël**

Fresh juvs show pale scaling on their upperparts

From below, Blue Petrels can be distinguished from prions by their darker heads and white undertails

From above, the white tail tip is diagnostic

Part of a large flock of Broad-billed Prions off Nightingale Island

PRIONS

Prions are the LBJs of the seabird world – although in this case they are 'little blue jobs'. These small, blue-grey petrels with a dark 'M' across the upperwing, dark tail tip and mostly white underparts are the most abundant seabirds in the Southern Ocean. They aggregate in huge flocks, extending over tens of kilometres, mainly at frontal zones, but also occur at lower densities virtually throughout the region. In sunlight, they are highly visible, as their white underparts stand out against the dark sea, but when it is grey and overcast – as is all too often the case – they disappear against the grey sea.

Prions are easily separated from other petrels – only the superficially similar Blue Petrel is likely to be overlooked among prion flocks – but species identification is very tricky, depending on subtle differences in head and tail patterns. The Fairy Prion is fairly straightforward to identify, but the remaining species form a continuum in bill size from Slender-billed to Broad-billed Prion. The extremes of this range are quite distinct, but with 5 species crammed along the continuum, many individuals cannot be identified at sea. The best approach is to photograph birds and then study their features from the images. Even in the hand, they can be hard to identify with certainty because there is overlap in the sizes of the different species.

All species breed in summer in burrows, rock crevices or caves. The timing of breeding is well synchronised, differing among similar species breeding at the same location (e.g. Broad-billed–Macgillivray's prions at Gough Island, and Salvin's–Antarctic prions at the Crozets). They are subject to occasional winter 'wrecks' when large numbers of dead and dying birds come ashore. The frequency of rare species is greater among beach-cast birds than birds at sea.

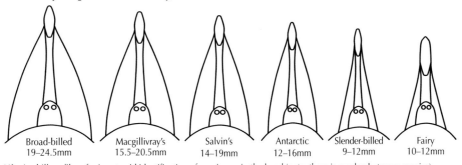

| Broad-billed | Macgillivray's | Salvin's | Antarctic | Slender-billed | Fairy |
| 19–24.5mm | 15.5–20.5mm | 14–19mm | 12–16mm | 9–12mm | 10–12mm |

Life-size bill profiles of prions to aid identification of specimens in the hand (note: there is overlap between species)

Fairy Prion *Pachyptila turtur*

24–26cm; 110–170g; bill width 10–12mm

The smallest prion and easiest to identify (at least if you ignore Fulmar Prion *P. crassirostris*, which is not known from the region) due to its broad black tail tip, plain face and short, dumpy bill. Some birds show a stronger supercilium, recalling Slender-billed Prion, but short bill and extensive black tail tip are diagnostic. **Voice:** Soft, cooing calls at colonies; usually silent at sea. **Status and biology:** Not threatened globally, but **NEAR THREATENED** in South Africa. 2 million pairs breed at sub-Antarctic islands, Tasmania and New Zealand, including 2,000 pairs at the Prince Edward Islands. Mainly breeds Oct–Feb; roughly 1 month earlier in N of range. Ads moult Mar–May; some return to colonies from Jun. Breeds in rock crevices, often in sea cliffs; regularly visits breeding cliffs during the day. In the African sector, typically remains south of 40°S, but ranges to 30°S in Australasia; winter vagrant to South Africa, where most records are of beached birds. Eats mainly small crustaceans.

Swartstertwalvisvoël

Underparts are often washed pale grey

The broad black tail tip is diagnostic

Fairy Prions have a rather plain head, short bill and extensive black tail tip

Slender-billed Prion *Pachyptila belcheri*　　25–27cm; 120–175g; bill width 9–12mm

Resembles Antarctic Prion (p.74), but with paler head, smaller, paler grey breast patches and a long, slender bill that is distinctive at close range. Head appears more rounded, recalling Fairy Prion, with a long, white supercilium that broadens behind eye, white lores, and narrow, blue-grey (not dark grey) cheeks. Black tail tip is reduced, with outer 3 tail feathers blue-grey (only 1 or 2 outer tail feathers lack dark tip in Antarctic Prion). In the hand, bill lacks palatal lamellae. Flight often more erratic than other prions. **Voice:** Silent at sea. **Status and biology:** 3 million pairs breed at sub-Antarctic islands, mainly Kerguelen and the Falklands/Malvinas. Breeds Nov–Feb; ads moult Mar–Apr, shortly after breeding, mainly in Antarctic waters SW of Africa. Rare visitor to shelf waters off sthn Africa, but large numbers irrupt in some years from normal range in sub-Antarctic and Antarctic waters. Eats crustaceans, fish and small squid; often takes larger prey than filter-feeding prions. Dunbekwalvisvoël

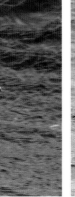

The blackish tail tip often protrudes

The bold white supercilium flares behind the eye

Slender-billed Prions have a bold white supercilium and narrow black tail tip, which appears as a narrow line on the undertail

Antarctic Prion *Pachyptila desolata*

25–28cm; 120–180g; bill width 12–16mm

By far the most abundant prion in sthn African waters. Bill is relatively narrow and typically distinctly bluish, but some black-billed birds occur; usually lacks black moustache behind gape and has a more striking facial pattern with a more prominent white supercilium and usually smaller breast smudges than larger species. Easily confused with Slender-billed Prion (p.73), but usually more robust with a heavier bill and more extensive black tail tip; in the hand, has palatal lamellae at the base of the bill. **Voice:** Deep, cooing calls at colonies; usually silent at sea, but occasionally calls in large flocks. **Status and biology:** 20 million pairs breed at sub-Antarctic islands and Antarctica in summer, most on South Georgia. Mainly breeds Dec–Apr; ads moult in late winter (Jul–Nov), but presumed imm birds moult Feb–Mar. Common non-br visitor to sthn Africa, occurring in large flocks. Eats mainly small crustaceans, filtered through baleen-like lamellae on sides of bill (hence alternative common name of 'whale-bird'). **Antarktiese Walvisvoël**

Antarctic Prion feeding

Rarely has a black bill

Antarctic Prions are the 'standard' prions seen off sthn Africa

The face pattern is quite variable

Salvin's Prion *Pachyptila salvini*

26–29cm; 130–210g; bill width 14–19mm

Intermediate in coloration and size between Macgillivray's (p.76) and Antarctic prions, but bill measurements overlap. Appears larger-headed than Antarctic Prion, with a steeper, more bulbous forehead, broader/deeper bill and typically has a blackish moustache curving up behind the gape. Bill bluer than in typical Broad-billed Prion (p.77), and moustache usually shorter. Most likely to occur in the Indian Ocean. **Voice:** Similar to that of Antarctic Prion.

Status and biology: Not threatened globally, but **NEAR THREATENED** in South Africa. 5 million pairs breed at Prince Edward Islands and Crozets. Thought to have evolved from hybrids between Antarctic and Broad-billed prions; mainly breeds Nov–Mar, roughly 1 month earlier than sympatric Antarctic Prions at Crozet. Ads moult Apr–May, shortly after breeding. Rare visitor to sthn Africa, but possibly overlooked. Fairly common in oceanic waters of the Agulhas Retroflection. Diet diverse, but eats mainly small crustaceans. Marionwalvisvoël

A head-on view is the best way to judge bill width

Juv has smaller bill than ad

Salvin's Prions breed only at the Prince Edward and Crozet islands; the head is more bulky than in Antarctic Prion

Macgillivray's Prion *Pachyptila macgillivrayi*   26–29cm; 150–220g; bill width 15.5–20.5mm

Recently described sister species to Broad-billed Prion; most on Gough Island but with a tiny relict population on St Paul Island, central Indian Ocean. Intermediate in size and structure between Salvin's (p.75) and Broad-billed prions; bill width overlaps with both species. Bill paler than in most Broad-billed Prions, with blue-grey sides and tip to bill, but this varies individually. Viewed from above or head on, sides of the bill are roughly parallel at the base, not widening to the base as in Broad-billed Prion. Probably not safely separable from Salvin's Prion at sea. **Voice:** Similar to that of Antarctic Prion. **Status and biology: ENDANGERED.** At least 100,000 pairs breed on Gough Island in sympatry with Broad-billed Prion; breed 2–3 months later than Broad-billed Prion but some evidence of gene flow; breeding success low due to predation of chicks by House Mice. In the Indian Ocean, <200 pairs survive on St Paul Island; extinct on Amsterdam Island. Ads from Gough mostly disperse S and W from Gough, but some ads from St Paul winter south of Africa. Breeds Nov–Feb; ads from Gough moult Mar–May in SW Atlantic. Eats copepods and other small crustaceans. Bloubekwalvisvoël

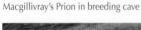
Macgillivray's Prion in breeding cave

Bill sides are parallel at the base

Macgillivray's Prion is very similar to Salvin's Prion

Broad-billed Prion *Pachyptila vittata*

27–30cm; 160–230g; bill width 19–24.5mm

The largest prion, with the broadest and darkest bill, but some individuals have bluish sides to bill, and exceptional birds have sides of the bill bright blue. Bill width overlaps with that of Macgillivray's Prion, but from above or head on, the bill widens right to the base. Appears very large-headed, with a steep forehead; whitish supercilium and dark grey face less well developed than in Salvin's Prion (p.75). Grey breast patches well developed. Blackish 'moustache' from gape typically curves up to join dark ear coverts. **Voice:** Similar to that of Antarctic Prion. **Status and biology:** Breeds at Tristan da Cunha and Gough Island (2–3 million pairs) and around New Zealand (1.5 million pairs). Breeds Aug–Dec; a few weeks earlier at Gough than at Tristan, possibly to reduce competition with sympatric Macgillivray's Prions. Ads moult in Nov–Feb, mainly in SW Atlantic, but a few moult S of Africa. Apparently a rare visitor to sthn Africa; stragglers often reach the region Apr–May, earlier than other prions. Eats mainly copepods and other small crustaceans, which are strained through 110–130 lamellae spaced 0.16mm apart on the sides of the upper mandible. Breëbekwalvisvoël

Bill broadens towards the base

Feeding by pumping water through its bill lamellae

Most Broad-billed Prions have blackish bills and well-defined black 'moustaches'

Kerguelen Petrel *Aphrodroma brevirostris* 33–36cm; 240–420g

A small, compact petrel recalling a *Pterodroma* petrel, but more closely related to fulmarine petrels. It appears large-headed with a thick 'bull-neck'; eyes large, often appearing hooded. Flight rapid and erratic with quick, stiff, shallow wing beats. Towers up to 50m above sea, often hanging motionless or fluttering kestrel-like. Smaller and greyer than Great-winged Petrel, with shorter, more rounded wings that show silvery highlights, especially on leading edge, and often extending onto breast. Most likely to be confused with rare dark-morph Soft-plumaged Petrel (p.80); best told apart by shorter, more rounded wings, heavier build and different flight action. **Voice:** Wheezy, high-pitched calls at colonies; silent at sea. **Status and biology:** Not threatened globally, but NEAR THREATENED in South Africa. 200,000 pairs breed on sub-Antarctic islands in summer; 100,000 pairs at Gough Island and 20,000 pairs at the Prince Edward Islands. Vagrant to sthn Africa; usually remains in sub-Antarctic and Antarctic waters south of 45°S but irrupts north in some years. Eats squid, crustaceans and carrion. Its large eyes contain more light receptors than the eyes of other albatrosses and petrels, suggesting that nocturnal foraging is important.

Kerguelense Stormvoël

The body often appears stubby due to the large, rounded head and fairly short tail

Head colour varies depending on the lighting, but this petrel usually shows silvery armpits

GADFLY PETRELS *PTERODROMA*

Medium-sized petrels characterised by erratic, towering and very rapid flight action. Bills dark; shorter and deeper than shearwaters and *Procellaria* petrels. Wings usually angled. No age or sex differences in plumage. All-dark species could be confused with Kerguelen, Mascarene, Jouanin's and Bulwer's petrels. Seldom occur close to shore unless there are strong onshore winds.

Great-winged Petrel *Pterodroma macroptera* 38–42cm; 460–700g

A dark brown petrel with a short, stubby, black bill. Wings long and slender, held angled at wrist. Wing and bill shape, dark (not silvery) underwing and short neck and bill differentiate it from Sooty Shearwater (p.96). Smaller than White-chinned Petrel (p.90), with black (not whitish) bill and gadfly jizz. Soars high above water in typical gadfly action, but flight tends to be more relaxed than that of other gadfly petrels. Recently split from Grey-faced Petrel *P. gouldi*, which has a more extensive pale face and heavier bill; records claimed from sthn Africa not supported by photographs or tracking data, which suggest that *P. gouldi* is confined to the Pacific Ocean. **Voice:** Loud, high-pitched screeching '*eeee, eeee di-di-di-di-di-di*' in flight at colonies; ground call is a high-pitched '*ki-ki-ki-ki*'; silent at sea. **Status and biology:** Not threatened globally, but NEAR THREATENED in South Africa. 250,000 pairs breed at sub-Antarctic islands in winter; 30,000 pairs at the Prince Edward Islands, where the population was hard hit by feral cats from 1950–1990. Once abundant at Tristan da Cunha and Gough Island, but numbers have decreased dramatically due to predation by introduced rats (Tristan) and mice (Gough); mice also kill chicks on Marion Island. Common non-br visitor to sthn Africa; most abundant in summer. Ads moult in midsummer, often appearing very scruffy. In calm weather roosts on the water in small flocks. Eats mainly squid, but scavenges at fishing boats if few other birds are present. Langvlerkstormvoël

Great-winged Petrels often sit on the water in calm weather

Flight feathers can appear silvery from below; upperparts are uniform, but show variable white patches when moulting

79

Soft-plumaged Petrel *Pterodroma mollis* 32–37cm; 240–360g

A small gadfly petrel with a variable dark breast band and white throat. White underparts contrast with grey underwings. Upperparts grey, with faint, darker 'M' across upperwings. Rare dark morph lacks silvery highlights of Kerguelen Petrel (p.78), has more slender neck, longer, more pointed wings, and longer tail. Flight rapid and erratic, with deep wing beats. Previously lumped with NW Atlantic *Pterodroma* petrels, which are now treated as 3 species: Fea's Petrel *P. feae* from the Cape Verdes (620 pairs), Bugio or Desertas Petrel *P. [f.] desertae* from the Desertas Islands (360 pairs), and Zino's Petrel *P. madeira* from Madeira (170 pairs). Claims of Fea's Petrel from sthn Africa based on birds lacking dark breast bands complicated by some Soft-plumaged Petrels lacking breast bands. Tracking data show ad Fea's Petrels are confined to the N Atlantic. Desertas Petrels winter off Brazil and may reach as far west as Tristan da Cunha; Zino's Petrels reach the tropical central Atlantic to 20°S, but both are very rare compared to Soft-plumaged Petrels. **Voice:** Ghostly '*oooo*' in flight at colonies; loud shrieks from burrows; silent at sea. **Status and biology:** Not threatened globally, but **NEAR THREATENED** in

South Africa. Perhaps 700,000 pairs breed at sub-Antarctic islands in summer, with roughly 500,000 pairs on Tristan/Gough (paler nominate race) and at least 15,000 on the Prince Edward Islands (darker *P. m. dubia*). Uncommon in shelf waters, appearing mainly when there are onshore winds; common offshore year-round. Eats mainly squid. **Donsveerstormvoël**

Wing shape changes dramatically when moulting (right)

Rare dark morph

Typical pale morph from below (left) and showing the dynamic flight action (right)

White-headed Petrel *Pterodroma lessonii*   40–45cm; 560–810g

A large, chunky gadfly petrel with a diagnostic whitish head and tail that contrast with the dark wings and back. Its large, dark eyes are accentuated by blackish feathering around them, contrasting with the pale head. Distinctly larger and more bulky than Soft-plumaged Petrel, with a heavier bill; lacks dark cap and breast patches, and has a plainer underwing, but best distinguishing features are the pale head and tail.

Voice: Silent at sea. **Status and biology:** Some 250,000 pairs breed at sub-Antarctic islands in summer, mainly off New Zealand but also at the Crozet and Kerguelen islands. May breed at the Prince Edward Islands; recorded ashore at night on both Marion and Prince Edward islands. Rare visitor to sthn Africa from oceanic waters; favours temperate waters from 10–20°C. Has become increasingly rare in the S Atlantic in recent years. Eats mainly squid; also crustaceans and occasional fish. Witkopstormvoël

From above, the whitish tail is diagnostic (left), but a few birds are darker with grey-mottled tails (right)

White-headed Petrels are larger and more heavily built than Soft-plumaged Petrels; underwing colour varies with lighting

Atlantic Petrel *Pterodroma incerta*

42–45cm; 450–680g

A large, brown gadfly petrel with a conspicuous white lower breast and belly. Much larger than Soft-plumaged Petrel (p.80), with chocolate-brown (not grey) plumage and much less distinct dark 'M' on upperwing. Given a poor view, could be confused with a pale-morph jaeger (pp.146–148). Larger and more heavily built than vagrant Trindade Petrel; best told apart by its dark underwing (lacks pale bases to its primaries and pale greater and lesser underwing coverts). Head usually all-brown with darker patches around eyes (lacking pale frons and throat of pale-morph Trindade Petrel), but in worn plumage, neck and mantle can appear mottled brown. Several dark and intermediate morph birds were collected on Gough Island in 1956. **Voice:** Loud, screeching calls given in flight at colonies, similar to, but deeper than those of Great-winged Petrel (p.79); silent at sea. **Status and biology: ENDANGERED.** Some 900,000 pairs breed on Gough in winter, where the chicks are heavily predated by introduced House Mice; in some years more than 80% are killed. A few pairs may persist at the main island of Tristan da Cunha (once a major population, but hunted for food and killed by introduced rats) and may breed in small numbers on the E plateau of Inaccessible Island. Disperses mostly west towards S America; vagrant to sthn Africa, although was locally common 200 miles south of the Cape in Nov 2002. Eats mainly squid; also some fish.

Atlantiese Stormvoël

Atlantic Petrel is a large, robust gadfly petrel with a heavy chest

Atlantic Petrel has a more uniform underwing than the rare Trindade Petrel

Trindade Petrel *Pterodroma arminjoniana* 38–40cm; 300–460g

A highly variable, mid-sized gadfly petrel with a slender body, squarish head and long wings and tail, characterised by the whitish bases to its flight feathers. Pale morph has white belly, recalling Atlantic Petrel, but is smaller with pale frons, throat and leading edge to underwing; upperparts brown with slightly paler greater coverts; lores usually dark. Could also be confused with vagrant Tahiti Petrel, but has broader, more angled wings, plain rump and less massive bill. Dark morph has brown underparts, including leading edge to underwing in some birds; usually retains some pale throat feathers but Round Island birds can have dark throat; most likely confused with larger Great-winged Petrel (p.79). **Voice:** Silent at sea. **Status and biology:** VULNERABLE. Some 2,200 pairs breed at Trindade and Martin Vaz islands off Brazil; 200 pairs on Round Island, Mauritius, where it hybridises with Kermadec *P. neglecta* and Herald *P. heraldica* petrels. Rare vagrant; one off Port Elizabeth in Jan 2014 probably from the Mauritian population (showed some characters of Herald Petrel and may be a hybrid); also observed at sea NW of Tristan da Cunha. Eats squid and fish. Trindadestormvoël

Dark morph from above and below; note very long, slender wings

Pale morph from above and below, showing more contrast in the underwing than Atlantic Petrel

Barau's Petrel *Pterodroma baraui*

38–40cm; 320–440g

The only gadfly petrel in the region with mostly white underwings. Larger than Soft-plumaged Petrel (p.80), with a darker cap and smaller grey breast patches. From a distance could potentially be confused with a *Calonectris* shearwater (pp.92–94), but smaller with different flight action; bill short and black. **Voice:** Silent at sea. **Status and biology: ENDANGERED.** 4,000 pairs breed in two main colonies 5km apart on Réunion, which are genetically distinct! It is threatened by introduced cats and rats, illegal hunting and light pollution, which causes fledglings in particular to crash land on their first flight to sea. Br ads winter mainly east of Réunion across to Australia from 15–30°S. Regular visitor to tropical east coast of sthn Africa, mainly in early summer; single records from the Cape and Namibia, and to 41°S. Eats squid and fish.

Baraustormvoël

The only gadfly in the region with mostly white underwings

Barau's Petrel is more slender than Soft-plumaged Petrel, with a darker face and crown

PSEUDOBULWERIA AND BULWERIA PETRELS

Small to medium-sized petrels; flight action generally less erratic and towering than gadfly petrels. Short, blackish bills are deeper than shearwaters and *Procellaria* petrels. Wings often held straight in *Pseudobulweria*; more angled in *Bulweria*. No age or sex differences in plumage. All-dark species could be confused with Kerguelen and Great-winged petrels (pp.78–79). Most species are Threatened and all are rare visitors to southern Africa.

Tahiti Petrel *Pseudobulweria rostrata* 38–40cm; 380–500g

A mid-sized brown petrel with a white belly; often shows some white streaking on the rump and variable paler centre to underwing. Superficially recalls a small Atlantic Petrel (p.82) or pale-morph Trindade Petrel (p.83), but undertail coverts are mostly white and has a different jizz; the long, thin wings are held straighter and often appear more blunt-tipped than in *Pterodroma* petrels. At close range the heavy black bill is diagnostic. **Voice:** Silent at sea. **Status and biology: NEAR-THREATENED.** Population poorly known; <10,000 pairs breed at islands in the S Pacific from New Caledonia to French Polynesia. Rare vagrant; one photographed off Durban in Nov 2018, adding credence to previous sightings from fishing vessels operating off sthn Mozambique in Nov–Dec 1987 and 1990. Eats squid and fish. Tahitistormvoël

At close range, the massive bill is distinctive

Plumage recalls Atlantic Petrel, but is more slender; wings held straight (not angled)

Mascarene Petrel *Pseudobulweria aterrima* 34–36cm; 180–260g

A blackish-brown petrel, most likely to be confused with Jouanin's Petrel, but slightly larger with a thicker neck and a relatively shorter tail. Lacks pale bar across upperwing coverts. Smaller than Great-winged Petrel (p.79) with longer neck, dark chin and uniform underwings. Long, slender wings are held straighter than Jouanin's or Great-winged petrel. Bill robust; almost as heavy as classic Jouanin's Petrel, and heavier than the slender-billed 'Jouanin's Petrels' seen in the Mozambique Channel. **Voice:** Silent at sea. **Status and biology: CRITICALLY ENDANGERED.** Some 100 pairs breed in two colonies on Réunion, where egg-laying differs by 2 months. Threatened by introduced predators and light pollution, which causes fledglings to crash land on their first flight to sea. Br ads winter across the Indian Ocean east to Australia. Status in the region poorly known: one tracked ad wintered off KZN and in the sthn Mozambique Channel. Eats squid and fish. Maskarenestormvoël

An all-dark petrel with long straight wings, thick neck and a heavy bill

Upperwing is uniform brown

Flight action is languid and wheeling

Jouanin's Petrel *Bulweria fallax*

30–32cm; 150–180g

Larger than Bulwer's Petrel (p.88), with proportionally shorter, square-tipped tail and different flight action; pale upperwing bar largely confined to the greater secondary coverts or absent. Has a longer neck than Bulwer's Petrel, heavier bill (although beware the smaller-billed 'Comoros' form) and less prominent pale upperwing bar that doesn't extend onto the wrist. Smaller than Mascarene or Great-winged petrels (p.79), but is smaller, with longer neck and tail; wings more slender. Long, pointed tail could cause confusion with noddies (pp.189–190), but it lacks pale crown, and bill is short and stubby. Usually seen in calm, tropical oceans, where it flies low over the water with long glides interspersed with rapid, deep wing beats. In windy conditions, arcs and wheels high over the waves with dynamic, gadfly-like flight. **Voice:** Silent at sea. **Status and biology:** NEAR THREATENED. Thousands of pairs breed at Socotra, off the Horn of Africa, and possibly at other sites around the coast of the Arabian Peninsula. However, most birds seen in the Mozambique Channel and around the Comoros have more slender bills than birds in the Arabian Sea and may represent an undiscovered breeding population (and possibly an undescribed species). Regular in the nthn Mozambique Channel mainly in early summer (Oct-Dec), when birds are in moult, but vagrant farther south. Eats small fish and squid. Donkervlerkkeilstert

Comoros petrels have smaller bills and often show a paler grey bar on the upperwing (fresh secondary coverts)

'Typical' Jouanin's Petrels from the Arabian Peninsula have a heavy bill and uniform upperwing

Bulwer's Petrel *Bulweria bulwerii*   26–28cm; 80–120g

The smallest petrel; dark brown with a diagnostic, long, wedge-shaped tail that is usually held closed and appears pointed. Superficially like a large all-dark northern storm petrel (pp.114–115), but has a deeper, stubby bill. Smaller than Jouanin's Petrel (p.87) with a shorter neck; usually has a more prominent pale grey-brown bar across the upperwing coverts that broadens towards the primaries (not confined to greater secondary coverts as in 'Comoros' form of Jouanin's Petrel). Flight is buoyant and graceful, gliding low over the water, but flaps faster and path more erratic than Jouanin's Petrel. **Voice:** Silent at sea. **Status and biology:** 100,000 pairs breed at islands in the N Atlantic and Pacific; small numbers off Mauritius. Rare Palearctic migrant to oceanic waters off the west coast, often associated with large flocks of Leach's Storm Petrels. Possibly regular in the tropical Indian Ocean and nthn and eastern Mozambique Channel Sep–Dec, but not yet recorded from sthn African waters in this area. Feeds by surface seizing; rarely dives (max 2–3m). Mainly eats lanternfish; also small squid, crustaceans and insects.
Bleekvlerkkeilstert

The smallest petrel in our region, Bulwer's is most likely to be confused with a large *Hydrobates* storm petrel

Typical Bulwer's Petrels are appreciably smaller than Jouanin's Petrel with a more extensive pale upperwing bar, but intermediate individuals in the SW Indian Ocean create a real identification challenge

PROCELLARIA PETRELS

The largest burrow-nesting petrels. Recall large shearwaters, but flight action is generally more relaxed and languid. Bill pale; fairly long, but deeper than those of shearwaters. No age or sex differences in plumage. All species often follow ships. Occasionally dive up to 20m, but mostly < 5m.

Grey Petrel *Procellaria cinerea*   48–50cm; 950–1,300g

The most distinctive *Procellaria* petrel, with pale, silvery-grey upperparts, white underparts, dark underwings and a yellowish bill. Grey-brown of head extends far down cheeks, with only narrow, white throat. At close range, ads and imms have distinctive mottled upperparts, created by old brown coverts and contour feathers dotted among new silvery-grey feathers. Also known as 'great grey shearwater' and could potentially be confused with a *Calonectris* shearwater (pp.92–94), but has dark grey (not white) underwing and mottled, not scaled, upperparts; lacks white rump band. **Voice:** Rattling and moaning calls at colonies; usually silent at sea. **Status and biology:** NEAR THREATENED globally, but VULNERABLE in South Africa. 100,000 pairs breed at sub-Antarctic islands in winter; 10,000 pairs at Gough Island and perhaps 6,000 pairs at the Prince Edward Islands. The population on Marion Island has shown little recovery since being hard hit by feral cats from 1950–1990; chicks are killed by mice at both Gough and Marion islands. Seldom ventures north of 40°S; rare visitor to sthn African waters. Eats squid, crustaceans and fish; sometimes scavenges from fishing boats; dives to 22m. Pediunker

The grey plumage blends into the Southern Ocean

The only *Procellaria* petrel with white underparts, it could be confused with a *Calonectris* shearwater

White-chinned Petrel *Procellaria aequinoctialis* 51–58cm; 1.0–1.6kg

The largest burrow-nesting petrel and the petrel most frequently encountered in most parts of sthn Africa. A large, blackish-brown bird with a whitish bill. At close range, shows a black 'saddle' to bill. Ad's bill is yellow-ivory; juv's pale grey. White throat is variable in extent – conspicuous in some individuals, but reduced or absent in others. Quite often has irregular white patches on head, belly or wings, but seldom has the Spectacled Petrel's distinctive white forehead. **Voice:** High-pitched trilling screams at colonies; often calls '*tititititititi*' when sitting in groups at sea. **Status and biology:** VULNERABLE. 2 million pairs breed at sub-Antarctic islands in summer, with largest populations on South Georgia and the Kerguelen Islands. About 50,000 pairs breed at the Prince Edward Islands, where numbers have increased following the eradication of feral cats on Marion Island in 1991. Southern African birds come from islands in the SW Indian Ocean, not from the large population on South Georgia. Ads moult Apr–Jul; imms in summer. Common year-round, but possibly decreasing due to accidental fishing mortality; it is the species most often killed by long-line fisheries in the Southern Ocean. However, has recovered well since cats were eradicated from Marion Island. Most abundant in shelf waters, where it scavenges at fishing boats. Often follows ships. Eats squid, crustaceans, fish and fishery wastes; dives to 16m. Facilitates capture of albatrosses on long-lines by bringing baited hooks to the surface, where they are stolen by larger albatrosses. Bassiaan

White-chinned Petrel ad outside its breeding burrow

White-chinned Petrels often rest on the water

As the most common petrel off sthn Africa, this species is the standard to which other species should be compared

Spectacled Petrel *Procellaria conspicillata* 50–56cm; 1.0–1.4kg

Similar to White-chinned Petrel, but with a diagnostic white spectacle and dusky bill tip. The size of the spectacle varies; incomplete in some birds, but always shows a diagnostic white forehead. Spectacle connected to white throat only in extreme individuals. Beware odd White-chinned Petrels with large white throats or white head markings, often on the crown or nape (but lack dusky bill tip). **Voice:** Trilling call at colonies similar to that of White-chinned Petrel, but also includes distinctive deep croaks and groans. Occasionally calls at sea. **Status and biology: VULNERABLE.** 14,000 pairs breed at Inaccessible Island, Tristan da Cunha, in summer, with numbers steadily growing following the disappearance of pigs from the island in the early 20th century. Probably also used to breed at Amsterdam Island, central Indian Ocean, but extinct there due to introduced predators. Rare visitor to sthn African waters year-round, but more common in summer, especially in oceanic waters. Attends trawlers and follows ships. Diet similar to that of White-chinned Petrel. Brilbassiaan

Spectacled Petrel outside its breeding burrow

Spectacle varies greatly; some have an eye-ring (inset)

Spectacled Petrels are easily overlooked in large flocks of White-chinned Petrels

SHEARWATERS

Small to medium-sized petrels, adapted for diving, using wings and feet underwater. Their name derives from their typical flight action, shearing low over the water with straight, stiff wings. Despite their relatively small wings, several species undertake trans-equatorial migrations.

Part of a raft of Great Shearwaters

Scopoli's Shearwater *Calonectris diomedea* 42–48cm; 420–720g

Recently split from Cory's Shearwater; smaller, with a finer bill, less extensive and greyer cap, paler mantle, and pale bases to the primaries on the underwing, but these characters are all subtle, and identification is complicated by individual differences and sex-linked variation in size. In the central Atlantic, care also is needed not to overlook Cape Verde Shearwater *C. edwardsii*, which is slightly smaller, with a slender, greyish bill with a black tip; tracking data indicate that this species reaches waters around Tristan da Cunha after wintering off Brazil before returning north. **Voice:** Silent at sea. **Status and biology:** 76,000 pairs breed at islands in Mediterranean. Occurrence off sthn Africa poorly known. Probably an uncommon Palearctic migrant to warmer waters off N Namibia; scarce farther south. Tracking

data show ad males remain mainly in the Canary Current off NW Africa; females travel farther south but winter mainly in the Angola Current. Sightings claimed from off the W Cape, but supporting evidence limited. Diet and foraging behaviour similar to that of Cory's Shearwater. **Scopolipylstormvoël**

Head averages paler and bill more slender than Cory's Shearwater

Very similar to more common Cory's Shearwater, but has paler bases to the underside of the outer primaries

Cory's Shearwater *Calonectris borealis* 46–50cm; 700–980g

Ash-brown above and white below with a large, yellow bill with a black tip. Only recently split from Scopoli's Shearwater; the two are very hard to tell apart. Cory's Shearwater is larger, with a more robust bill, more extensive and browner cap, less contrast between the mantle and upperwings, and fully dark primaries on underwing (but this is tricky to see and dependent on light conditions). Lacks dark cap of Great Shearwater (p.95); upperparts paler, but can show pale crescent at base of tail. Flight is slow and languid on broad wings; stays close to water, not banking and shearing as much as other shearwaters. **Voice:** Silent at sea. **Status and biology:** 126,000 pairs breed at islands in N Atlantic and W Mediterranean. Common Palearctic migrant to warmer waters off sthn Africa. Eats mainly fish; often forages in association with dolphins and game fish. Dives usually shallow (mostly <1m; max 5m); takes some prey in the air. Geelbekpylstormvoël

Cory's Shearwater on the water

White underwings separate it from Grey Petrel

Often appears darker faced than Scopoli's Shearwater; dark underside of primaries can appear paler in bright light

Streaked Shearwater *Calonectris leucomelas* 44–48cm; 450–700g

Similar to Scopoli's (p.92) and Cory's (p.93) shearwaters, but with white face and streaked crown, nape and cheeks, and blue-grey bill with a darker tip (consider also Cape Verde Shearwater). Underwing coverts finely streaked, appearing darker than coverts of Cory's Shearwater, especially on primary coverts. **Voice:** Silent at sea. **Status and biology: NEAR THREATENED.** Breeds at islands in NW Pacific; migrates to seas off SE Asia, New Guinea and Australasia. Very rare vagrant to KZN, Aug–Oct; one record from the W Cape. Eats mainly fish and squid. **Gestreepte Pylstormvoël**

Darker primary underwing coverts are diagnostic

Bill is duller than Cory's or Scopoli's shearwaters

May show some white on rump

Head pattern is quite variable, but always has whitish area around eye

Great Shearwater *Ardenna gravis*

45–51cm; 750–1,100g

A dark-capped shearwater with a diagnostic dark belly patch (variable in extent), pale nuchal collar and broad white rump. Darker above than *Calonectris* shearwaters (pp.92–94), with blackish cap and dark bill; flight action more direct, with faster wing beats and straighter wings. Underwing is mostly white, with indistinct dark lines across the axillaries and underwing coverts. **Voice:** Hysterical, staccato wailing at colonies, like crying babies; usually silent at sea, but calls extensively in rafts offshore of breeding islands. **Status and biology:** Some 4–5 million pairs breed at Tristan da Cunha (Nightingale and Inaccessible islands) and Gough Island, with a small colony on the Falklands/Malvinas. Breeding density so great locally that some pairs lay eggs on the ground beneath dense tussock grass. Common mainly on passage off sthn Africa, especially Sept–Oct and Mar–Apr, but present in smaller numbers throughout summer; rare in winter. During incubation, some ads visit the Benguela, but most forage on the Patagonian Shelf. Often joins flocks of other shearwaters (especially Sooty Shearwater) and attends fishing vessels. Sometimes killed for stealing baits from tuna pole boats, but very seldom caught on long-lines in sthn Africa. Eats mainly fish, including fishery wastes; also squid and crustaceans; dives to 19m. Grootpylstormvoël

Great Shearwater landing

Great Shearwaters often rest on the water

The dark cap, scaled upperparts and white rump are diagnostic; the size of the dark belly patch varies among individuals

Sooty Shearwater *Ardenna grisea*   40–46cm; 680–960g

A brown shearwater with diagnostic pale, silvery underwing centres (intensity varies with light conditions). Bill long, slender and dark. Narrow, pointed wings are held straight, with little bend at wrist. Flight intersperses rapid bursts of flapping with short glides, but becomes more looping and petrel-like in strong winds. Main ID challenge is separating from rare Short-tailed Shearwater, although could also be confused with vagrant Balearic Shearwater (p.100). **Voice:** Silent at sea. **Status and biology: NEAR THREATENED.** Some 5 million pairs breed at sub-Antarctic islands in summer, mostly off New Zealand and sthn S America; a few pairs have bred at Tristan da Cunha. Most of the population migrate to the northern hemisphere in winter. Common in coastal waters year-round off sthn Africa, but most abundant May–Sept. Eats small fish, crustaceans and fishery wastes; dives to 70m (but most dives much shallower); generally uses partly closed wings for propulsion. Malbaartjie

Typical Sooty Shearwater on the water

On take-off, the silvery underwing centres are clearly visible

Atypical bird with grizzled pale head

Toes can extend past tail tip

Prominent pale underwing bar is whitest on primary underwing coverts

Longer bodied than Short-tailed Shearwater

Short-tailed Shearwater *Ardenna tenuirostris*   40–44cm; 550–900g

Easily confused with abundant Sooty Shearwater; averages slightly smaller and more slender, with a shorter bill, steeper forehead, less marked silvery underwings and shorter tail (toes often extend beyond tail tip in flight, but this can also be shown by some Sooty Shearwaters). The shorter bill and rounded head give it a more petite, gentle jizz. **Voice:** Silent at sea. **Status and biology:** Some 6 million pairs breed at islands off Tasmania and SE Australia. Migrates to the N Pacific in winter. Breeding birds regularly reach the central Indian Ocean at around 60°S, and at least occasionally irrupt farther west, reaching the central S Atlantic around Bouvet Island. A few migrate north in the Atlantic Ocean. Only one confirmed record from sthn African waters, off the Cape in Aug 2014. Eats small fish, crustaceans and fishery wastes. Kortstertpylstormvoël

Appears more petite than Sooty Shearwater

Short-tailed Shearwaters often travel in large flocks, careening over the water

Appears more compact than Sooty Shearwater

Underwing has paler centre, but is more uniform than in Sooty Shearwater

Often appears to have a darker cap

97

Flesh-footed Shearwater *Ardenna carneipes*   45–50cm; 550–680g

A dark brown shearwater with a dark-tipped, flesh-coloured bill and flesh-coloured legs and feet. Larger winged than Sooty Shearwater (p.96); lacks silvery underwing, but has pale primary bases; flight is more petrel-like, with wings more bent at wrist. Smaller than White-chinned Petrel (p.90); bill is pinkish with a darker tip. Shorter, more rounded tail and pale bill, legs and feet distinguish it from Wedge-tailed Shearwater. **Voice:** Silent at sea. **Status and biology: NEAR THREATENED.** 220,000 pairs breed at south-temperate islands in Indian Ocean, and off Australia and New Zealand in summer. Uncommon visitor to sthn Africa year-round, mainly off the east coast. Occasional birds recorded ashore on Dyer Island in Sep–Oct. Eats fish, squid and fishery wastes; dives to 27m. **Bruinpylstormvoël**

Resembles a small White-chinned Petrel

Bill is heavy for a shearwater

Tail is shorter than in Wedge-tailed Shearwater

Lacks pale centre to underwing

Wedge-tailed Shearwater *Ardenna pacifica*   40–45cm; 320–500g

A slender shearwater with a long, graduated tail that appears pointed in flight. Flight is light and buoyant on broad wings, held bowed forward and down. Plumage polymorphic. Mostly dark-morph birds recorded from African waters – dark brown all over, with dark bill, legs and feet (unlike Flesh-footed Shearwater). Pale morph is brown above and white below, with clear-cut cap. Superficially resembles Great Shearwater (p.95), but lacks pale rump and nape and has a longer tail and different flight action; underwing is more mottled brown. **Voice:** Ghostly wailing at colonies; silent at sea.

Status and biology: 100,000 pairs breed at tropical and subtropical islands in the Indian and Pacific oceans. Rare visitor to tropical east coast; occasional birds come ashore and call at night on islands in Algoa Bay. Eats mainly fish and squid; often feeds in association with game fish and other predators. Keilstertpylstormvoël

Seldom fans its wedge-shaped tail

Bill is less pink than in Flesh-footed Shearwater

Pale morph is rare off sthn Africa

Often glides with angled wings   Long tail is distinctive

Dark morph in moult

Balearic Shearwater *Puffinus mauretanicus*

32–38cm; 420–550g

Formerly considered a race of Manx Shearwater, but is larger, with brown (not black) upperparts; lacks sharp contrast on face. Typically has dark axillaries and dusky underparts and underwings, although this is variable. Some individuals are almost all-dark, resembling a small Sooty Shearwater (p.96). **Voice:** Silent at sea. **Status and biology:** CRITICALLY ENDANGERED. 3,000 pairs breed at the Balearic Islands, Spain; total population perhaps 25,000 birds based on migration surveys. Most remain north of the equator, with females moving farther south than males. At best a rare vagrant to sthn Africa; only a few records from the west coast, with no compelling photographic evidence. Eats small fish and squid. **Baleariese Pylstormvoël**

Bill averages heavier than Manx Shearwater's

Underwing pattern less well defined than Manx Shearwater's

Averages larger than Manx Shearwater and often appears more pot-bellied

Browner above than Manx Shearwater

Underparts variable; some browner birds could be confused with Sooty Shearwater

Manx Shearwater *Puffinus puffinus*

30–38cm; 350–520g

The largest black-and-white shearwater in the region, with a relatively long, slender bill and pointed wings. Black upperparts usually contrast with white underparts; often has white bands onto sides of rump; undertail coverts white. Black cap extends below eye, with pale 'C' on ear coverts. Flight action comprises glides interspersed with rapid beats of stiff, straight wings, similar to Sooty Shearwater (p.96), not like rapid, fluttery flight of Little/Subantarctic shearwaters (pp.103–104). **Voice:** Silent at sea. **Status and biology:** 300,000 pairs breed at islands in temperate N Atlantic; most winter off Brazil, but some reach sthn Africa, where it is uncommon in shelf waters, mostly Oct–Apr; occurs in oceanic waters on migration. Often found among Sooty Shearwater flocks. Eats mainly fish. Swartbekpylstormvoël

Subtle pale 'C' behind ear coverts

Sitting at sea (often with other shearwaters and petrels)

Browner individual in heavy primary moult

Upperparts usually appear blackish

Crisply defined underwing pattern with black flight feathers

Baillon's (Tropical) Shearwater *Puffinus bailloni*   28–32cm; 150–250g

A small black-and-white shearwater; intermediate in bill size, wing shape and flight action between Little/Subantarctic (p.104) and Manx (p.101) shearwaters. Lacks pale 'C' extending onto ear coverts of Manx Shearwater; plumage more contrasting black and white (but can appear dark brown when worn). Formerly lumped with other races of 'tropical' shearwater, but now generally considered to be an endemic species confined to the SW Indian Ocean. Told from other species in the complex by its mainly white undertail coverts. **Voice:** High-pitched, squeaky call at breeding colonies; silent at sea. **Status and biology:** Confined to Europa Island (100 pairs) and Réunion (4,000 pairs). Persian Shearwater *P. persicus temptator* (500 pairs at the Comoros) and Seychelles Shearwater *P. nicolae* (up to 100,000 pairs at tropical islands from the Seychelles to the Maldives) may also reach the region. Fairly common in tropical and subtropical waters off the east coast, ranging farther south than previously thought. Eats mainly small fish. Tropiese Kleinpylstormvoël

Lacks white 'C 'on face of Manx Shearwater

Broad black trailing edge to wing

Worn greater coverts are browner

Structure intermediate between Manx and Little-type shearwaters; white undertail separates from Persian and Seychelles shearwaters

Little Shearwater *Puffinus assimilis*

25–30cm; 120–200g

The only small black-and-white shearwater with white coloration of the face extending above the eyes, but in harsh light Subantarctic Shearwater (p.104) can appear white faced. Tiny; slightly smaller than Subantarctic Shearwater, but structure and flight action similar. Smaller and shorter-billed than Baillon's or Manx (p.101) shearwaters. Wings short and rounded with a narrow black trailing edge and mostly white leading edge to underwing. **Voice:** Silent at sea. **Status and biology:** 40,000 pairs of *P. a. tunneyi* breed at islands off Western Australia; at least 100,000 pairs of other races breed in the temperate Pacific from Lord Howe to the Kermadec islands. Scarce visitor to warmer oceanic waters, mainly associated with the Agulhas Retroflection region. One occupied a burrow on Bird Island, Algoa Bay, in May 1978. Most records are from Jan–Jul. Eats fish, squid and crustaceans. Kleinpylstormvoël

Sits on the water fairly often

Usually blacker above than Subantarctic Shearwater

Underwing has narrow black trailing edge

Slender necked compared to Subantarctic Shearwater; head often raised slightly in flight

103

Subantarctic Shearwater *Puffinus elegans* 25–30cm; 180–290g

Recently split from Little Shearwater (p.103). A tiny, black-and-white shearwater with silvery highlights on its upperparts. Distinctive flight action alternates rapid wing beats with short glides. Structure and flight action very similar to that of Little Shearwater, but has dusky (not white) face. Smaller than Baillon's Shearwater (p.102) and with a shorter bill, dusky (not clean-cut) facial pattern and mainly white underwing, lacking a black elbow line. Appreciably smaller and shorter-billed than Manx Shearwater (p.101); wings short and rounded with narrow black trailing edge to underwing (similar in width to leading edge, not twice as wide, as in Manx Shearwater). **Voice:** High-pitched, trilling '*whit-it-it-it-it*' at colonies; silent at sea. **Status and biology:** Population poorly known; roughly 200,000 pairs, mainly at New Zealand sub-Antarctic islands; perhaps 10% at Tristan da Cunha and Gough Island. Numbers at Gough have decreased dramatically in recent years due to mouse predation of chicks. Fairly common in oceanic waters, especially in winter, but only a rare visitor to coastal waters, mostly May–Sept. Eats fish, squid and crustaceans.

Sub-antarktiese Pylstormvoël

Flapping occurs in rapid bursts

Face can appear white in bright light

Upperparts appear silvery-grey in sunlight (left) but darker on dull days (right)

Underwing is mostly white

A large flock of Wilson's Storm Petrels feeding with a White-chinned Petrel in the wake of a fishing boat

STORM PETRELS

Storm petrels are the smallest seabirds, with some weighing less than 20g. They appear out of place as they flutter around at sea far from land. The 28 species are divided between 2 families; the 10 southern storm petrels (Oceanitidae: *Oceanites, Garrodia, Pelagodroma, Fregetta* and *Nesofregetta*) are characterised by long legs and a hopping gait and are an ancestral lineage to the albatrosses and petrels, whereas the 18 northern storm petrels (Hydrobatidae: now all in one genus, *Hydrobates*) walk on their shorter legs and are more closely related to the petrels.

Storm petrel flight involves more flapping than the dynamic soaring of albatrosses and petrels, but they have extremely large wings relative to their body mass, giving them low wing loadings. This allows them to fly slowly, often into the wind, making good use of the ground effect close to the water surface. They also use their feet to run, dance or even ski (*Fregetta*) on the water. They capture most prey by surface pattering, but they can dive to half a metre or so if necessary. At close range they presumably detect prey visually, but rely on scent at larger spatial scales, and are strongly attracted by fish oil and chum.

The sexes look alike, and juveniles lack distinct plumages. Like the petrels, they are monogamous, and lay a single white egg (spotted pink in some species) in a burrow or rock crevice. Nests can be very hard to find; the breeding grounds of several S American species remain undiscovered. The parents share incubation duties, but may leave the egg unattended for days at a time with no ill effect (but increasing their susceptibility to introduced mice). The semi-altricial chicks are fed by regurgitation. Adults cease feeding their chicks before they fledge, and disperse widely after breeding; several species undertake trans-equatorial migrations.

Of the 28 species, 9 are globally threatened but 3 southern species are so poorly known that they are listed as Data Deficient. There is also one recently extinct species. The main threat to most species is habitat loss and the introduction of mammal predators to their breeding islands. Feral cats eradicated storm petrels from Marion Island, and they are only now recolonising the island. House Mice have greatly reduced their populations on Gough Island. Most species accumulate large amounts of ingested plastic.

White-faced Storm Petrel *Pelagodroma marina* 19–21cm; 40–60g

A pale, very long-legged storm petrel with diagnostic white underparts and a prominent white eye-stripe. Brown above with paler upperwing coverts; rump pale grey. Flight is erratic, with jerky wing beats; long toes extend well beyond tail tip. When feeding, it hovers and bounds over the water, pushing off with its feet. **Voice:** Mournful cooing at colonies; silent at sea. **Status and biology:** Roughly

1 million pairs breed at temperate islands in the NE Atlantic, S Atlantic and around Australasia in summer; at least 20,000 pairs breed at Tristan and Gough Island, but numbers at Gough have decreased due to mouse predation. Tristan birds apparently disperse north; seldom seen east of the islands. All records at sea Apr–May; regular in the Mozambique Channel; vagrant elsewhere. One caught ashore on Dyer Island in Oct 2001. Eats small crustaceans and fish.

Witwangstormswael

White underparts and striking head pattern are diagnostic

Note the exceptionally long legs and toes

Pale bars across coverts and whitish rump

Individual with very worn wing feathers

Grey-backed Storm Petrel *Garrodia nereis*   15–18cm; 30–40g

A tiny storm petrel with a black head and breast merging into a blue-grey back, rump and upperwing coverts. Belly and underwing coverts white. Lacks white rump of White-bellied Storm Petrel (p.109). Easily overlooked as it ghosts away from ships, matching the lead-grey sea. **Voice:** Soft, cricket-like call at colonies; silent at sea. **Status and biology:** Not threatened globally, but **NEAR THREATENED** in South Africa.

50,000 pairs breed at sub-Antarctic islands; perhaps 5,000 pairs at Gough Island where numbers are greatly reduced by mouse predation. At least 1,000 pairs breed at the Prince Edward Islands; extirpated from Marion Island by cat predation, but recently discovered breeding again 30 years after cats were eradicated. Rare vagrant to sthn Africa; typically remains south of 40°S, usually fairly close to breeding islands. Eats mainly larvae of goose barnacles, and often forages at drifting kelps. Grysrugstormswael

MARK YATES

Recalls tiny White-bellied Storm Petrel

Flying slowly with legs dangling

The only white-bellied storm petrel without a white rump; uniform grey back and black tail tip are diagnostic

107

Black-bellied Storm Petrel *Fregetta tropica* 19–21cm; 45–60g

Fregetta storm petrels are fairly large, chunky storm petrels with a characteristic flight action, gliding over the waves, seldom flapping, and regularly kicking up a line of spray with one foot or the breast; however, they do not ski over the water in calm conditions. Both species have a broad white rump, white underwings and mostly white belly. Black-bellied has a brown back, matching upperwing coverts; lacks prominent grey-scaling on coverts of nominate White-bellied Storm Petrel found in the Indian Ocean. Nominate race has a black line down the central belly (rarely incomplete), linking the black breast and vent, although this can be hard to see, especially in harsh light. *F. t. melanoleuca* from Tristan da Cunha and Gough Island has a white belly; see White-bellied Storm Petrel for separating characters. Very rare dark morph has entire underparts black. **Voice:** High-pitched, whistled '*peeeee*' at colonies; silent at sea. **Status and biology:** Not threatened globally, but **NEAR THREATENED** in South Africa. Some 150,000 pairs breed at sub-Antarctic islands in summer; at least 5,000 *F. t. tropica* at the Prince Edward Islands and perhaps 50,000 pairs of *F. t. melanoleuca* at Tristan da Cunha and Gough Island, but numbers at Gough greatly decreased due to predation by introduced House Mice. Most migrate north into tropical waters in winter. Fairly common passage migrant off sthn Africa Apr–May and Aug–Oct. Eats small crustaceans, fish, squid and fishery wastes. Attends trawlers; sometimes follows ships. Swartpensstormswael

Fregetta storm petrels often bound off the water (left), sometimes skiing over the surface (right)

Nominate Black-bellied Storm Petrel (left to right): above, below and side on, when the black belly is often hard to see

Black-bellied Storm Petrel

Black-bellied   White-bellied

ID not black and white

The discovery that Black-bellied Storm Petrels with white bellies breed on Tristan and Gough has greatly complicated the identification of *Fregetta* storm petrels in the S Atlantic. The two species breed together at Tristan's uninhabited islands.

White-bellied Storm Petrel *Fregetta grallaria*   19–21cm; 45–65g

Similar to Black-bellied Storm Petrel, but belly is all-white. Birds of nominate race, mainly seen in the Indian Ocean, are fairly easily identified by their pale greyish back (due to grey-edged coverts) that contrasts with brown upperwing coverts. However, birds from the Tristan da Cunha Archipelago have brown backs and are very hard to distinguish from white-bellied *F. t. melanoleuca* race of Black-bellied Storm Petrel that also breeds at Tristan and Gough Island. In the hand, combination of longer wings and shorter legs is diagnostic. In the field, toes barely project beyond tail tip in flight (longer in Black-bellied) and birds have some dusky tips to white rump feathers (pure white in Black-bellied); black vent U-shaped (not square-across) and birds lack white throat patch shown by some *F. t. melanoleuca*. **Voice:** Apparently similar to Black-bellied Storm Petrel, but calls at Tristan unknown. **Status and biology:** Some 100,000 pairs breed at south-temperate islands; largest population at Tristan. Very rare over the African continental shelf. *F. g. grallaria* is scarce in oceanic waters, mainly in the Agulhas Retroflection in summer. Status of *F. g. leucogaster* from Tristan in sthn African waters unknown. Seldom follows ships. Eats small crustaceans, fish and squid.
Witpensstormswael

Darker-backed *F. g. leucogaster* is easily confused with Black-bellied Storm Petrel   Nominate race (top, above)

Wilson's Storm Petrel *Oceanites oceanicus*

15–19cm; 25–40g

A fairly small, dark storm petrel with a broad, white rump that wraps around onto the flanks. Legs long; toes project beyond tail in flight; often dangle below bird when it is feeding by dancing over water, but can be retracted into belly plumage. Yellow toe webs are very hard to see. Can show a paler bar on underwing when moulting, but usually not as well marked as the white underwing stripe of smaller European Storm Petrel; tail appreciably longer, and square-tipped (not rounded); legs much longer; wings broader and more rounded. Flight is swallow-like and direct, with frequent glides, but flight action varies with wind strength. Less erratic than flight of European Storm Petrel, but flaps more than Band-rumped and Leach's storm petrels (pp.112–113). Photographs of birds with white extending onto the vent or belly and with a white underwing bar may be Fuegian race *O. o. chilensis* or possibly even Pincoya Storm Petrel *O. pincoyae*. **Voice:** Silent at sea. **Status and biology:** 6 million pairs breed at sub-Antarctic islands and Antarctica, including Bouvet and the Crozets during summer; often seen feeding close inshore at Prince Edward Islands and occasionally caught ashore, so may breed there too. Common visitor to shelf waters off sthn Africa; less abundant in oceanic waters. Occurs year-round; more common in winter than summer, but is most abundant during passage, especially from Mar–May, but also Sep–Oct. Often follows ships. Eats crustaceans, small fish, squid and fishery wastes. Gewone Stormswael

Usually lacks white underwing bar

Yellow toe webs are seldom visible

Longer tailed than European Storm Petrel, with protruding toes

Feeds by dancing on the water

European Storm Petrel *Hydrobates pelagicus* 14–18cm; 20–32g

Slightly smaller and darker than Wilson's Storm Petrel, with a short, rounded tail and diagnostic white underwing bar; pale bar on upperwing coverts less pronounced and flight action typically more rapid and fluttery. Legs short; toes do not project beyond tail tip in flight. **Voice:** Wheezy, nasal calls at colonies; silent at sea. **Status and biology:** 500,000 pairs breed in the NE Atlantic from Iceland and Norway to the Canary Islands; <20,000 pairs in the Mediterranean Sea. Genetic evidence suggests that the small Mediterranean population *H. [p.] melitensis* is distinct, and might be split in future; it breeds about a month earlier than the nominate race, has different calls, and apparently starts breeding at the age of 1–2 years (4–5 in most nominate birds). The two races are indistinguishable at sea; it is not known whether Mediterranean birds reach sthn Africa. Common Palearctic migrant to sthn Africa from Oct–May, mostly over the continental shelf. Often gathers in large flocks at trawlers; patters over water when feeding. Occasionally roosts on the water, normally in small flocks. Diet similar to that of Wilson's Storm Petrel. Europese Stormswael

A tiny, compact storm petrel with white underwing bars

Legs shorter than Wilson's Storm Petrel; do not protrude beyond tail tip despite shorter, rounded tail

Leach's Storm Petrel   *Hydrobates leucorhous*   19–22cm; 30–50g

Larger than Wilson's and European storm petrels (pp.110–111), with a long, forked tail and narrow, V-shaped white rump. Best identified by its long wings and languid flight action, gliding low over waves with wings held forward and bent at wrist, flapping infrequently. Wing beats deep, causing erratic changes in direction. White rump usually divided by dusky central line; rarely all grey-brown. **Voice:** Rhythmical chattering and trilling at colonies at night; silent at sea. **Status and biology:** VULNERABLE globally, but CRITICALLY ENDANGERED in South Africa. 8 million pairs breed in the N Atlantic and N Pacific; up to 20 pairs used to breed at guano islands off W Cape, but currently <10 pairs following predation by vagrant owls (Dassen Island). Fairly common, singly or in small groups, in oceanic waters, mostly Oct–Apr. Tracking studies show birds from NE Canada visit sthn Africa. Roosts on water in calm weather, often with Great-winged Petrel (p.79). Seldom follows ships. Eats small crustaceans, fish and squid.

Swaelstertstormswael

Note pale wing bars and divided white rump

Wings usually held angled forward with bent wrist (left), but can be straighter when banking; tail fork obvious except when fanned (right)

Band-rumped Storm Petrel *Hydrobates castro* 20cm; 35–50g

Intermediate in size and structure between Wilson's (p.110) and Leach's storm petrels. Flight action closer to that of Leach's Storm Petrel, but it is more dumpy with shorter, broader wings, a larger white rump patch, less prominent upperwing bars and a less deeply forked tail (appearing almost square when fanned). Legs short; toes do not extend beyond tail tip in flight.

Status and biology: Some 46,000 pairs breed at temperate and tropical islands in the Atlantic and N Pacific oceans south to St Helena. Systematics complicated by summer- and winter-breeding forms at many islands, and the Cape Verde population is distinct from other Atlantic populations. Often split into 3 or 4 species, but no reliable characters to identify them at sea. Rare vagrant to sthn Africa; only one confirmed record from Lüderitz (affinity unknown). Madeirastormswael

White rump wraps further onto sides than in Leach's Storm Petrel

Straighter winged than Leach's Storm Petrel, with only shallow tail fork; note variable upperwing bar

113

Swinhoe's Storm Petrel *Hydrobates monorhis* 20cm; 38–45g

A fairly large, all-dark storm petrel with long, broad wings and a prominent pale bar across the upperwing coverts. Size and flight action similar to that of Leach's Storm Petrel (p.112); told from rare dark-rumped Leach's Storm Petrel by its straighter wings that appear more rounded, less pronounced pale upperwing bars that do not reach the leading edge of the wing, and by its larger head with a heavier bill. Smaller and shorter-tailed than Matsudaira's Storm Petrel; white bases to primary shafts much less prominent (seldom visible at sea). **Voice:** Silent at sea. **Status and biology: NEAR THREATENED.** Perhaps 20,000 pairs breed at islands off Japan; probably also in NE Atlantic. Non-breeders disperse south into the tropical Indian Ocean, preferring warmer waters than Matsudaira's Storm

Petrel. Very rare vagrant to sthn Africa, mainly to oceanic waters off the east coast in spring; all-brown storm petrels seen off N Namibia might also be this species. Eats small crustaceans, fish and squid. Swinhoestormswael

Pale upperwing bars are often subdued

Note angular head and short legs

Pale bases to outer primary shafts visible only at close range

Resembles an all-dark Leach's Storm Petrel, but with straighter wings

Matsudaira's Storm Petrel *Hydrobates matsudairae* 25cm; 60–65g

A very large, all-dark storm petrel with long, broad wings and a prominent pale bar across the upperwing coverts. Appreciably larger and longer-winged than Swinhoe's Storm Petrel, with a longer, more deeply forked tail and proportionately smaller head. The bases of the outer primaries are white, forming a distinctive pale patch when viewed from a distance. Similar in size to Bulwer's Petrel (p.88), but tail forked (not wedge-shaped). **Voice:** Silent at sea. **Status and biology:** VULNERABLE. Perhaps 5,000 pairs breed at islands south of Japan; non-breeders disperse south into the tropical Indian Ocean, preferring cooler waters than Swinhoe's Storm Petrel. Very rare vagrant, mainly from the tropical east coast, May–Jul, with one record off Cape Point. Eats small crustaceans, fish and squid.

Oosterse Stormswael

White primary bases are prominent when the bird is feeding   Appears small-headed compared to Swinhoe's Storm Petrel

Long tailed with a deeper tail fork and usually more prominent pale wing bar than Swinhoe's Storm Petrel

115

DIVING PETRELS

The diving petrels have traditionally been placed in a separate family (Pelecanoididae), but genetic evidence suggests that they are highly modified petrels. Traditionally, 4 species are recognised, 2 confined to South America, and 2 more widespread around the Southern Ocean, but the relict population of diving petrels on Whenua Hou (Codfish) Island, south of New Zealand, has recently been split from South Georgia Diving Petrel, and further splits are possible within Common Diving Petrel.

Like the northern hemisphere auklets, diving petrels specialise in eating small crustaceans, and also have a gular pouch to store food. Even their plumage bears a striking resemblance to the very abundant Little Auk *Alle alle*. These chunky little birds are wing-propelled pursuit divers that attain impressive depths (>60m) for such small birds. Their short wings are adapted for flight under water, so they have to flap very rapidly to stay airborne, buzzing low over the water. At least some individuals become flightless during moult.

They are reputed to fly through rather than over waves, but it isn't clear whether or not they really fly through the waves. They do often resort to diving into the water.. As the series of photographs shows, their landings can be less than elegant. Their high flight speed also renders them prone to killing themselves if they collide with ships or buildings after being disoriented by lights at night.

There are no obvious age or sex differences in plumage. Their breeding biology is typical of the petrels; all species breed in burrows and lay a single white egg. They are unusual among petrels in being able to re-lay following breeding failure, and may breed as early as one year of age. Of the 5 species, 2 are globally threatened. Like other petrels, they face threats at the breeding sites (habitat loss, disturbance and introduced predators), but they are also susceptible to gillnet fishing. Populations of both species on Marion Island are slowly recovering following the eradication of cats, which caused the local extinction of Common Diving Petrels.

Swimming away from an approaching ship

Sequence showing a Common Diving Petrel hitting a wave and crashing into the sea

Common Diving Petrel *Pelecanoides urinatrix* 20–25cm; 110–170g

Very hard to separate from South Georgia Diving Petrel at sea, but typically appears more chunky with a larger head and bill; underwing dusky (not white) and white trailing edge to secondaries reduced or absent. In the hand, the long, stout bill has more or less parallel rami when viewed from below; paraseptal processes in nostrils are located closer to the head (not central). **Voice:** Querulous '*wooee-wip*' at colonies; silent at sea. **Status and biology:** Not threatened globally, but **NEAR THREATENED** in South Africa. 7 million pairs breed at sub-Antarctic islands, SE Australia and New Zealand in summer; 35,000 pairs at Tristan da Cunha and Gough Island; 10,000 pairs at the Prince Edward Islands; recently discovered breeding again at Marion Island after being extirpated by introduced cats.

Some remain close to breeding sites year-round, but tracked birds from South Georgia dispersed east after breeding to winter NE of Bouvet; observations at sea suggest some diving petrels from Prince Edward disperse southwest, but a few observed northwest of islands within 1,100km of S Africa. One beached specimen from Cape Town in Mar 2021 was first continental African record. Eats small crustaceans; dives to 64m. Gewone Duikstormvoël

Note dusky head and face, and dark-tipped secondaries

South Georgia Diving Petrel *Pelecanoides georgicus* 18–22cm; 90–150g

Slightly smaller than Common Diving Petrel. Hard to identify at sea; typical birds have more obvious white line on scapulars, white trailing edge to secondaries and greater coverts (dark in Common Diving Petrel), and cleaner white underparts (dusky breast and underwing in Common). Often shows a well-marked face, with paler C around darker ear coverts. In the hand, has a smaller bill with arched rami when viewed from below; and a black line along rear of leg. **Voice:** Squeaky calls at colonies; silent at sea. **Status and biology:** Not threatened globally, but **NEAR THREATENED** in South Africa. 6 million pairs breed at sub-Antarctic islands in summer; perhaps 5,000 pairs at the Prince Edward Islands. Non-breeding dispersal little known, but birds from South Georgia disperse east after breeding to winter NE of Bouvet. Not recorded from sthn Africa. Eats small crustaceans; dives to 49m. Kleinduikstormvoël

Note the pale tips to the secondaries and whitish 'C' behind the ear coverts

117

Ad Red-tailed Tropicbird showing its relatively small paddle-like feet

TROPICBIRDS

Traditionally, the 3 species of tropicbird (Phaethontidae) were placed in the Pelecaniformes with the cormorants, gannets, frigatebirds and pelicans because all 4 toes in all these groups are webbed (only 3 toes webbed in other waterbirds). However, genetic evidence shows that tropicbirds are the most distinct lineage of seabirds and they are now placed in their own order.

As their name suggests, tropicbirds are confined to tropical waters, where they feed mainly well offshore by plunge-diving. They have robust bills with serrated edges and surprisingly small wings for their size, making them flap almost continuously, with a characteristic stiff-winged flapping action. They typically fly 10–50m above the sea, where presumably they detect their prey visually, and also cue in on foraging groups of other marine predators such as dolphins or tunas. All foraging appears to occur during the day, and they roost on the water at night. Legs and feet are almost vestigial; they shuffle awkwardly on the ground.

The sexes are alike, but they have distinct juvenile plumages, which gradually moult into adult plumage over 2–3 years. Adults have elongate central tail streamers, which explains their Afrikaans name *pylstert*. Like other seabirds, they are monogamous, and pairs may remain together

at sea. All lay a single egg in a sheltered crevice or under vegetation, either on offshore islets or on steep, inaccessible cliffs. Eggs are unusual in being tan or rufous-brown. They can re-lay if the first egg is lost. Both sexes incubate and feed the semi-altricial chick, regurgitating food by inserting their bill into the chick's gullet. Juveniles receive no further assistance from their parents after fledging.

All 3 species are widespread, and none is globally threatened, but many populations have decreased due to human disturbance and hunting, habitat loss and the impact of introduced predators.

White-tailed Tropicbird in nest cavity

White-tailed Tropicbird   *Phaethon lepturus*   35–40cm (plus 35–45cm streamer); 260–400g

The smallest tropicbird; two-thirds the size of the 2 red-billed species. Ads have diagnostic orange-yellow bills, neat black facemasks and extremely long, wispy, white or golden tail streamers (shafts black). In flight, they have 2 black patches on each wing; one on the outer primaries and one across the median coverts – the latter absent from other tropicbirds. Ads from Europa Island (*P. l. europae*) have an apricot wash over the underparts. Juv lacks long tail streamers and has barred upperparts and a pale yellow-grey bill with a darker tip. Bill paler than juv Red-tailed Tropicbird's (p.120), wings less uniformly barred, but with black outer primary patch and heavily marked median coverts of ad; primary coverts all white (lacking black feather shafts of juv Red-tailed). Told from juv Red-billed Tropicbird (p.121) by its smaller size, more slender build, longer, more pointed wings, lack of a nuchal collar and less extensive black panels in outer primaries. **Voice:** Loud '*kek kek kek*' at colonies; silent at sea. **Status and biology:** Global population poorly known; perhaps 50,000 pairs breed at tropical islands worldwide, including 2,200 pairs at Ascension Island, S Atlantic, and 1,000 pairs at Europa Island, Mozambique Channel. Sometimes split into 2 species, with Catesby's Tropicbird *P. catesbyi* confined to the Caribbean and adjacent N Atlantic. The Europa Island population is closer genetically to the S Atlantic population than other colonies in the W Indian Ocean. Lays 1 egg in a shallow scrape. Regular in oceanic waters of the Mozambique Channel; rare farther south off the east coast and off the west coast, but is perhaps regular well offshore off N Namibia. Eats fish and squid Witpylstert

Sub-ad retains some barring on its back and rump

Ad showing diagnostic black bar across wing coverts, which is visible even from below (inset)

119

Red-tailed Tropicbird *Phaethon rubricauda*   45–50cm (plus 30–35cm streamer); 600–760g

A large, pale tropicbird. Ad is mostly white (tinged pink when breeding), with a red bill and red tail streamer (but this can be hard to see at a distance). Tertials have black centres; otherwise black on the wing is confined to the shafts of the primaries and primary coverts in the outer wing, appearing white from a distance. Juv lacks tail streamers; easily confused with other juv tropicbirds, but has a blackish bill with a dull red or dark grey base (not pale, yellowish base), and upperparts are more uniformly barred above, with less black in the outer primaries and with black feather shafts to the primary coverts (not all white). Juvs gradually lose barring over 2–3 years, with imms appearing intermediate between juvs and ads. **Voice:** Various cackling and croaking calls given at colonies; generally silent at sea, but occasionally gives a deep '*kraak*', similar to that of a Caspian Tern (p.169). **Status and biology:** Global population poorly known; perhaps 30,000 pairs breed at tropical islands in the Indian and Pacific oceans. At least 3,000 pairs breed at Europa Island, Mozambique Channel; 100 pairs at Nosy Ve, SW Madagascar. Tracked birds from these colonies feed mainly in the Mozambique Channel and south of Madagascar to 34°S; rare off the east coast of South Africa to the W Cape; vagrant inland. Occasional individuals visit cliff sites and offshore islands, sometimes returning repeatedly for days or weeks. In South Africa, most frequently recorded at Bird Island, Algoa Bay. Lays 1 egg in a shallow scrape. Eats fish and squid, including flying fish and flying squid. **Rooipylstert**

Ad (top) and fledgling (bottom) on breeding island

The palest tropicbird; ads appear white from a distance, and juvs have less black in their primaries than other species

Red-billed Tropicbird *Phaethon aethereus* 45–55cm (plus 45–50cm streamer); 700–800g

The largest tropicbird. Ad has a red bill and white tail streamers; easily told from Red-tailed Tropicbird by its finely barred back, which appears grey at a distance, extensive black panels in the outer wing, and by its long, white (not red) tail streamers. At close range, has a longer black eye-stripe, which sometimes extends across the nape in worn plumage. Males' tail streamers average longer than those of females. The NW Indian Ocean race *P. a. indicus* not known to reach the region; averages smaller with a more orange bill; could be confused with White-tailed Tropicbird (p.119), but has finely barred back and upperwing coverts (not white with a broad black band across the upperwing coverts). Juvs lack tail streamers and are heavily barred above; bill yellow, sometimes with a dusky tip; black eye-stripes extend onto the nape to form a nuchal collar. Best told from juv Red-tailed Tropicbird by its paler bill and more contrasting upperwing pattern, with extensive black outer primaries contrasting with the all-white greater primary coverts. Larger and heavier than juv White-tailed Tropicbird, with broader, more rounded wings. **Voice:** Occasional piercing screams at sea. **Status and biology:** Global population poorly known; fewer than 10,000 pairs breed at tropical islands in the E Pacific and Atlantic oceans as well as around the Arabian Peninsula in the NW Indian Ocean; latter population sometimes treated as a separate species, Arabian Tropicbird *P. indicus*. Some 1,200 pairs of the nominate race breed at tropical islands in the S Atlantic, mainly on Ascension Island. Very rare vagrant to oceanic waters off the west and south coasts of sthn Africa. Eats fish and squid. Rooibekpylstert

Ad on breeding island

Ad has large black panel in outer wing and barred back, appearing grey from a distance

121

Ad male Great Frigatebird with his deflated gular sac barely visible

FRIGATEBIRDS

The 5 species of frigatebird (Fregatidae) are an unusual family within the Suliformes, together with the gannets, cormorants and darters. These large, tropical, pelagic seabirds are unique among seabirds in lacking waterproof feathers, and rarely, if ever, land on the water. They obtain all of their food on the wing – famously by stealing food from other birds, but more usually by picking prey from the sea surface, or catching flying fish and flying squid in flight. As a result, frigatebirds are the most aerial of seabirds, and arguably of all birds.

They achieve this remarkable aerial prowess thanks to their extremely long, angled wings and large, deeply forked tails, coupled with a very light skeleton, which together confer a very low wing loading and high agility. Remarkably, their feathers weigh more than their entire skeleton. Their low wing loading allows them to fly slowly, averaging less than 20km/h. They have tiny feet, used only for perching on the trees or shrubs where they typically nest. However, all 4 toes are still partly webbed, indicating a once more

aquatic lifestyle. Their long, hook-tipped bills are ideal for snatching up slippery prey.

Frigatebirds soar effortlessly, rising hundreds of metres above the sea using thermals or trade winds, and then glide down when they spot a feeding opportunity. Occasionally they enter large cumulus clouds, where the powerful updrafts carry them up at 4–5m per second to heights of more than 4,000m. Heart rate monitors and accelerometers show that they expend least energy when soaring at about 500m, and work harder when close to the surface, where turbulence is greater, and they flap more while foraging. They seldom drop to sea level at night, when they spend about 5% of the time sleeping, although usually only resting one half of their brain at a time.

The sexes differ both in plumage and size, with females larger than males. Plumage also varies with age, birds taking 5 years to attain adult plumage, greatly complicating their identification. Adult males tend to be mostly glossy black and have naked red throat pouches. The pouches are inconspicuous most of the time, but are inflated hugely to create bizarre balloon-like structures when they display. Females, immatures and juveniles typically have some white on the head or breast, with the location and extent varying subtly among species, and within populations of the same species. Sex-related differences in plumage are evident from the third year. Primary moult is protracted, with several active moult centres. At least some populations suspend moult while breeding.

Frigatebirds are monogamous and may retain the same mate in successive years. All species lay a single egg, usually in a stick platform built in a tree or shrub, but they will nest on the ground in areas lacking vegetation. Both sexes incubate and feed the semi-altricial chick by regurgitation. Breeding is protracted, taking 7–8 months from laying to fledging (similar to a small albatross). And even then the parents' job is not done. Juveniles return to their breeding island every night for 5–10 months after fledging, where they are fed by their parents, allowing them to attain their independence gradually. As a result of this very long breeding cycle, pairs typically raise at most 1 chick every 2 years.

Once the apron strings are finally cut, the juveniles head off on a long aerial excursion. Juvenile Great Frigatebirds from Europa Island disperse into the tropical Indian Ocean, travelling around the edge of the monsoon belt, avoiding the areas where hurricanes spawn as well as the doldrums over equatorial waters. They remain aloft for up to 2 months at a time, only occasionally touching down on tropical islets such as the Seychelles, Maldives and Chagos archipelagos.

Of the 5 species, 2 are globally threatened, including the vagrant Christmas Frigatebird. The main threats are deliberate hunting for food, accidental bycatch on fishing gear, predation by introduced predators and disturbance of breeding sites. Neither of the species breeding on Europa Island is currently at risk, but frigatebirds rely heavily on other marine predators, especially tunas, to drive their prey to the surface. As a result, they probably are adversely affected by heavy fishing pressure on tunas in tropical waters.

Imm frigatebirds, like this Lesser Frigatebird, exhibit a complex series of age- and sex-related plumages

Great Frigatebird *Fregata minor*

86–104cm; 700–1,500g

Underwing wholly dark in all plumages, lacking the white 'armpits' of Lesser and most Christmas (p.126) frigatebirds. Ad male is glossy black, with a paler brown bar across its upperwing coverts, and reddish feet. Ad female has white breast and throat, grey chin and red eye-ring and feet. Juv has whitish or tawny head and throat, dark breast band and white lower breast and forebelly; can show white armpit spurs in some populations, but told from juv Lesser Frigatebird by rounded (not triangular) white belly patch. Imm white from chin to belly, gradually darkening with age. **Voice:** Various whistles and shrieks at colonies; also makes vibrating and clapping noises with its bill; male holds its bill against its inflated throat pouch to enhance bill rattling. Silent at sea. **Status and biology:** Some 100,000 pairs breed at tropical islands in the Indian and Pacific oceans, and locally at islands off Brazil. 1,000 pairs breed at Europa Island; regular in Mozambique Channel, rare farther south; vagrant inland, usually after cyclones. Lays 1 egg in a flimsy stick nest built in a tree or shrub. Ads from Europa fly on average 180m above the sea, descending to feed mainly in the early morning and evening; virtually no feeding occurs at night. During incubation, ad foraging trips typically last 4–7 days, travelling up to 600km from Europa,

right across the Mozambique Channel, but most head west towards Mozambique. Trips during the brood period are shorter (1 or 2 days), and tend to head northwest to around Bassas da India. Some failed breeders remain in the Mozambique Channel, returning to the island every 5–10 days, but some disperse, with one bird reaching Aldabra (Seychelles), 1,570km away, only a day after leaving Europa. After breeding, ads and fledglings disperse into the tropical Indian Ocean, landing sporadically at other islands. Eats fish and squid, especially flying fish and flying squid. Grootfregatvoël

Ad male with deflated throat pouch

Imm Great Frigatebird left; dark breast band grows with age; ad female right

Lesser Frigatebird *Fregata ariel* 70–82cm; 650–950g

Smaller and more angular than Great and Christmas (p.126) frigatebirds, but size is hard to assess on lone birds. Ad male glossy black with diagnostic white 'armpits' extending from axillaries to sides of breast; pale upperwing bars less marked than in other male frigatebirds; feet dull red-black. Ad female has white breast, the coloration extending as collar onto neck; feet red and eye-ring red or blue; differs from female Great Frigatebird by black throat and white breast with white spurs extending to the armpits; from female Christmas Frigatebird by black belly extending up centre of breast. Juv has brownish head, black breast and white belly that is typically narrower and more pointed than in juv Christmas Frigatebird. Imms typically have dark (brownish or black) throat, more extensive black on belly, and white breast, with white extending to armpits. **Voice:** Similar to that of Great Frigatebird. Silent at sea. **Status and biology:** Some 50,000 pairs breed at tropical islands in the Indian and west central Pacific oceans, and locally at islands off Brazil. The W Indian Ocean *F. a. iredalei* breeds at 3 sites only – Aldabra, St Brandon's Reef and Europa

Island, Mozambique Channel, where some 1,200 pairs breed. Foraging ecology presumably similar to that of Great Frigatebird, but has not been studied. Rare off east coast, seen mostly after summer cyclones. Lays 1 egg in a flimsy stick nest built in a tree or shrub. Eats fish and squid, especially flying fish and flying squid. Unlike Great Frigatebirds, seldom if ever attempts to steal food from Red-footed Boobies (p.129) returning to Europa Island. Kleinfregatvoël

Sub-ad female

Ad male showing diagnostic white 'armpits'

Juv differs from juv Great Frigatebird in having white belly extending onto its underwing; inset: ad female

Christmas Frigatebird *Fregata andrewsi* 86–104cm; 700–1,500g

A large frigatebird with a white belly in all plumages. Ad male black with white belly, extending onto 'armpits' in some birds. All other plumages have white armpits, which average broader based than in Lesser Frigatebird (p.125). Ad female has white belly extending onto breast and armpits; contrasting with black head, chin and throat, and rounded black spurs on either side of the breast. Juv has mottled brownish head and upper breast separated from white belly by black spurs on sides of the breast; best told from juv Lesser Frigatebird by broader, more extensive white belly patch and typically narrower black band across central breast. Imm has whitish head, gradually darkening with age; usually has prominent black spurs on either side of the breast. **Voice:** Silent at sea. **Status and biology:** CRITICALLY ENDANGERED; some 1,000–2,000 pairs breed at Australia's Christmas Island, S of Indonesia. The population continues to decrease due to the impacts of phosphate mining at Christmas Island and bycatch at sea, including deliberate targeting for food. Mostly confined to SE Asia, from Indonesia and Malaysia to the Philippines, but vagrants wander more widely to N Australia, China and occasionally farther west in the Indian Ocean, reaching India and Kenya; one record from the coast of KZN in January 2022. Witpensfregatvoël

Ad male

Ad female

Young imm

Imm male; inset shows younger imm from above

Juv showing buffy head

Cape Gannets pursue a school of sardine during the sardine 'run' off the Eastern Cape

GANNETS AND BOOBIES

The 10 species of gannets and boobies (Sulidae) form the Suliformes with the frigatebirds, cormorants and darters. Traditionally 2 genera have been recognised – the larger gannets *Morus* and the smaller boobies *Sula* – but genetic evidence shows that Abbott's Booby, now confined to Christmas Island, is ancestral to all other species, and it is placed in a separate genus, *Papasula*. Most boobies have tropical ranges, whereas the 3 gannets breed only in temperate areas. However, fossil remains of several extinct gannets have been found in tropical areas, indicating that they once had a wider distribution.

Gannets and boobies are the largest plunge divers, using the momentum of flight to carry them to their underwater prey. Adaptations to this foraging technique include the absence of external nares (opening into the mouth) and large subcutaneous airsacs that absorb the impact of hitting the water at speeds of up to 100km/h. However, these birds are so streamlined that they experience very little resistance as they enter the water, descending at 3–4m/s to surprise their prey. Gannets use their momentum to reach prey <10m

deep, but use their wings and feet to pursue prey to greater depths. Boobies typically dive from lower heights at more oblique angles, and probably obtain most of their prey close to the surface.

The large mass of gannets imparts considerable momentum as they plunge vertically from heights of up to 30m. This can be hazardous when hundreds of birds dive onto a school of fish at the same time. Video footage of the sardine 'run' shows that nearly 1% of dives result in a collision with a gannet or another predator. This can prove fatal; gannets have been found with deep puncture wounds in their heads and necks consistent with being hit by another gannet.

Although gannets and boobies plunge from considerable heights, their commuting flight is typically low over the water, thus taking advantage of the ground effect, alternating bouts of flapping and gliding. Their heart rate is 20% higher when flapping than when gliding. They save energy by flying in lines to slipstream the lead bird, each bird flapping and gliding in the same place, but with the lead bird flapping slightly more often than its followers.

Adult gannets are highly conspicuous at sea thanks to their mostly white plumage, which facilitates detecting feeding groups from considerable distances. Tracking studies show that birds change direction and increase their flight speed to join foraging groups up to 40km away. Birds leaving colonies also head in the direction of returning birds, increasing their chances of finding feeding groups.

The sexes are alike in size and plumage, but differ in the coloration of bare parts in some boobies. Juvenile plumage is distinct, the birds taking 2–4 years to attain adult plumage. Moult is protracted, with multiple active centres in the primaries (termed Staffelmauser or stepwise moult). Pairs often retain the same mate in successive years, and both sexes incubate and feed the altricial chick. They lay 1–3 (rarely 4) eggs, but seldom raise more than 1 chick. If the clutch is lost early in the season, a replacement clutch can be laid. They lack a brood patch, incubating with their feet. Most species breed on the ground, but Abbott's and Red-footed boobies breed in trees or bushes. The altricial chicks are fed by regurgitation. The fledging period varies greatly in boobies, depending on food supply. Gannets provide no further parental care once the chicks fledge, but booby chicks continue to be fed for 4–6 weeks.

Of the 10 species, 2 are globally threatened, including the Cape Gannet (Endangered). The main threats to Cape Gannets are competition with commercial fisheries for food, accidental bycatch on fishing gear and disturbance of breeding sites. Predation by Cape Fur Seals is particularly worrying. At Malgas Island, 30–80% of fledglings are killed by seals as they rest on the water around the island, and increasing attacks on adults on the island threaten the entire colony. At Lambert's Bay, fur seal attacks on adults ashore caused the entire colony to abandon the site in 2005; only swift and sustained action against the seals saw the gannets return the following year. Disease such as avian 'flu is another concern, with outbreaks in 2022 greatly impacting Northern Gannet populations.

Cape Gannets plunge-dive onto a surfacing hake trawl net

Red-footed Booby *Sula sula*

66–77cm; 900–1,200g

A small, slender booby with a long, pointed tail. Ad has bright red legs and a blue bill with a pink base; eye dark in most birds, but some golden. Plumage polymorphic; almost all ads on Europa Island are white-tailed brown, but white morph dominant in Seychelles colonies. Brown morph is much smaller than juv gannets, and has plain (not speckled) plumage. White morph has yellow wash on head like an ad Cape Gannet (p.132), but much smaller and white tail and black carpal patches on underwing are diagnostic. Juv is streaked brown, with grey-brown bill and greyish-yellow feet. Imm white morph is mottled white and brown. **Voice:** Noisy at colonies, where both sexes give harsh '*karrk*' calls; sometimes calls to other birds while foraging. **Status and biology:** 350,000 pairs breed at tropical islands worldwide. Resident around Europa Island, Mozambique Channel, where some 3,500 pairs breed; scarce farther south along the east coast. Tropical Atlantic population smaller, with 1,300 pairs at Fernando de Noronha, Brazil; vagrant to west coast, occasionally visiting gannet colonies. Typically return to land in the evening, irrespective of whether they are breeding or not. Br ads from Europa feed only during the day, and do not rest on the water at night; commute at about 40km/h (max 95km/h); range up to 150km from the island. Clutch invariably 1 egg, laid in a stick nest in tree or shrub canopy. Eats flying fish and squid. Often perches on ships' masts; hunts prey flushed by the vessel. Birds returning to Europa are kleptoparasitised by Great Frigatebirds (mainly females, which are larger than males) and Brown Skuas. Boobies reduce the risk of losing meals by flying higher, travelling in groups, and returning to the island as late as possible. Rooipootmalgas

Imm perched on ship's mast

Ad white-tailed dark morph

Ad white morph

Ad brown morph

Imm pale morph

Masked Booby *Sula dactylatra*

80–90cm; 1.4–2.2kg

A large white booby with golden eyes and a small black facial mask. Lacks yellow head of ad Cape Gannet (p.132) and has broader black secondaries extending to body. Black (not white) tail and dark (not red) legs separate it from smaller, white-phase Red-footed Booby (p.129). Juv has mottled brown head, back and rump; resembles Brown Booby, but has narrow white hind neck collar, less extensive brown on breast, and more white on underwing with a dark central bar (clearly defined, smaller white area in Brown Booby; juv Red-footed Booby has all-dark underwings). **Voice:** High double honk; generally silent at sea. **Status and biology:** Breeds at tropical islands in the Atlantic, Indian and Pacific oceans; global population poorly known – perhaps 5,000 pairs in S Atlantic, <1,000 pairs in the W Indian Ocean. Numbers have decreased due to disturbance and exploitation for food. Rare vagrant to sthn Africa, recorded once off the east coast and once south of Cape Agulhas. Eats mainly fish. **Brilmalgas**

Ad on breeding island

Ad showing black mask and black humeral feathers

Juv showing dark grey head and distinctive striped underwing

Juv (left) and ad (right)

Imm could be confused with imm Cape Gannet

Brown Booby *Sula leucogaster*

64–74cm; 900–1,500g

Ad is dark brown with a white lower breast and belly, and a broad white underwing panel. Bill pale grey, washed blue-green; legs yellowish. Uniform upperparts and crisply defined white underparts distinguish it from juv gannets (pp.132–133). Juv is duller brown above; has brown flecks on white belly, but lacks white speckling of juv gannets. Differs from juv Masked Booby by uniform brown upperparts and well-demarcated (not fuzzy) underpart pattern. **Voice:** Silent at sea. **Status and biology:** Breeds at tropical islands worldwide; global population at least 50,000 pairs, but likely decreasing. Vagrant to both the west and east coasts from breeding islands in the tropical S Atlantic (main colonies on Ascension Island and St Paul's Rock) and W Indian Ocean (where it is the rarest booby; perhaps 200 pairs breed on Cosmoledo Atoll, Seychelles, and islets off NW Madagascar). Records from the west coast have all been of birds ashore in gannet colonies, whereas most records from the east coast have been storm blown, associated with the passage of tropical cyclones. Eats mainly flying fish and squid. Forages in coastal waters more than other boobies. Bruinmalgas

Some juvs are all brown

Ad showing well-defined underpart pattern

Ads on breeding island

Imm showing yellowish feet

Imm showing clean-cut breast band

Cape Gannet *Morus capensis*

84–95cm; 2.3–3.1kg

Ad white with yellow wash on head, and black tail and flight feathers; some have 1–4 white outer tail feathers. Juv is brown with white spots, whitening gradually, typically starting with the head. Juv could be confused with Brown Booby (p.131), but is larger and lacks clear-cut brown bib and white belly. Males have slightly longer gular stripes than females, but with extensive overlap. **Voice:** Noisy '*warrra-warrra-warrra*' at colonies and when feeding. **Status and biology:** Br endemic. **ENDANGERED** globally and in South Africa; **CRITICALLY ENDANGERED** in Namibia, where numbers crashed following the collapse of sardine stocks in the early 1970s. 130,000 pairs breed in dense colonies in spring and summer at Mercury, Possession and Ichaboe islands off sthn Namibia (13,000 pairs), Lambert's Bay and Malgas Island off the W Cape (27,000 pairs) and Bird Island, Algoa Bay (90,000 pairs). Large numbers follow the sardine run along the east coast to KZN in winter; others migrate to Gulf of Guinea; occasional vagrant to Amsterdam and St Paul islands, central Indian Ocean, and to Australia. Lays 1 egg (rarely 2) in a guano mound on the ground. Eats mainly pelagic fish (sardine, anchovy, saury, red-eye, maasbanker), but also fishery wastes. Plunge dives to 10m (swims to 22m). Foraging diurnal; rests on water after feeding to digest meal. Ads provisioning small chicks feed up to 300km from breeding islands, travelling at 40–50km/h (max 115km/h). Different colonies have largely non-overlapping foraging ranges – birds from Malgas Island forage south to Cape Agulhas, but seldom venture more than 50km north into St Helena Bay, which is the preserve of gannets from Lambert's Bay. **Witmalgas**

Imm typically moults head and neck first

Atypical ad with white outer tail feathers

Juv averages darker than juv Australasian Gannet

Australasian Gannet *Morus serrator*

83–92cm; 2.0–2.8kg

Similar to Cape Gannet; ad has greyish eyes, a darker golden head and a shorter gular stripe; outer 3 tail feathers white, but some Cape Gannets have 1–4 white outer tail feathers. Juv averages paler below than juv Cape Gannet, but can only be identified with certainty by its short gular stripe. Most records are of birds at gannet colonies, where they are best located by their higher-pitched call. **Voice:** Higher pitched than Cape Gannet's. **Status and biology:** 75,000 pairs breed in New Zealand and SE Australia; a few pairs on St Paul Island. Vagrant to sthn Africa; some 30 individuals recorded at Cape Gannet colonies. Hybridises with Cape Gannet in Africa and SE Australia. Eats mainly small fish. **Australiese Malgas**

Ad Cape (left) and Australasian (right) gannets

Sub-ad with black tail and scattered black wing feathers

Juv showing whitish underparts

Ad from above; imm taking off (inset)

Juv from above

133

White-breasted (left) and Cape (right) cormorants are sthn Africa's two most widespread marine cormorants

CORMORANTS AND SHAGS

The cormorants and shags are a rather uniform family (Phalacrocoracidae) that occur worldwide. They range in size from the Little Cormorant (430g) to the Flightless Cormorant (males up to 4kg). Their taxonomy remains unresolved, with 35–41 species placed in up to 7 genera. Some species are found mainly in freshwater habitats, but most occur in the sea at least sporadically.

Cormorants are the best exponents of foot-propelled diving. All 4 toes of their large feet are webbed, their tails are stiff to aid steering underwater, and their legs are positioned far back on the body for optimal propulsion. Most feed on the seabed, using their long, sinuous necks to probe crevices, or to shoot out and grab fish, squid or other prey with their hook-tipped bills. Small prey is swallowed underwater, but large prey is brought to the surface where it is juggled until it can be swallowed head first. The cormorants' gape and gullet can expand greatly, but occasionally their enthusiasm exceeds their ability and they either abandon the attempt or choke trying to swallow too large a fish.

Cormorants diving in deep water jump at the start of a dive, whereas those feeding in shallow water do not. This is because dive angles tend to be steeper when diving in deeper water to minimise the time spent commuting to and from the seabed. Diving efficiency, defined as the ratio of dive time to recovery time on the surface, typically is greater than one for aerobic dives, but much lower for anaerobic dives.

Some species swallow stones to reduce their buoyancy while diving, and thus increase their diving efficiency. However, the main mechanism used by all cormorants is their partly wettable plumage, which reduces the amount of air trapped in their feathers. This comes at a cost, however, as it reduces their insulation, restricting them to short foraging bouts. Most species have to return to land to warm up after an hour or so at sea – and in the case of Great Cormorants feeding in the frigid waters off Greenland in winter, foraging bouts last less than 10 minutes.

Only a few species are able to rest on the water for several hours and thus exploit pelagic prey far from land. All are found in upwelling regions where pelagic schooling fish are abundant – Guanay Cormorants in the Humboldt system, Cape Cormorants in the Benguela, and Socotra Cormorants in the Arabian Sea. These species also undertake much longer foraging flights than other cormorants, travelling in flocks to locate their patchy prey.

The sexes look the same, but males average slightly larger. All species have bare skin on the throat or face, which is more brightly coloured in the pre-breeding period, when many species also have short-lived plumage features (e.g. white filoplumes on the head). Juveniles are typically duller and paler, acquiring adult plumage over 1–4 years. Primary moult is protracted, with multiple active moult centres in older birds (termed wave moult or Staffelmauser).

Cormorants usually lay 2–4 eggs, but occasionally up to 7; replacement eggs can be laid if the clutch is lost. They breed colonially, building nests of vegetation on islands, cliffs, or in trees or reedbeds at wetlands, often associated with herons and ibises. They incubate with their feet, and the altricial chicks are fed by regurgitation. Juveniles continue to be fed at the colony for a few weeks or even months after fledging.

Of the 34 extant species recognised by the IUCN, 11 are globally threatened and 2 are Near Threatened. Pallas's Cormorant from the Bering Sea, was hunted to extinction around 1850. 2 of the 3 cormorants endemic to southern Africa are Endangered. The main threats include competition with fisheries for food, climate change, disease outbreaks and disturbance of their breeding grounds.

Crowned Cormorant chicks vie for attention

Bank Cormorant incubating on its nest built from seaweeds

Cape Cormorant *Phalacrocorax capensis*

60–65cm; 900–1,600g

An all-dark marine cormorant; smaller and more slender than Bank Cormorant, with paler gular skin. Often occurs in large flocks; flies over the sea in long lines, hence the Afrikaans name *Trekduiker*. Br ad glossy black with chrome-yellow gular patch, turquoise eyes and banded turquoise-and-black eye-ring; non-br ad has duller bare parts. Juv brown, with paler underparts; almost whitish in some birds; eye-ring and gular skin grey-brown.
Voice: Nasal grunts and croaks, mainly at colony.
Status and biology: ENDANGERED. Near-endemic, breeding from S Angola to Algoa Bay. Numbers have decreased 60% over last 40 years; currently 100,000 pairs, with largest population on Dyer Island (up to 38,000 pairs). Main threats are outbreaks of avian cholera as well as competition with the pelagic fishery for food off the west coast. Foraging trips of ads provisioning chicks average 3–4 hours from west coast colonies, 1.3 hours from Dyer Island. More aerial than other cormorants; br ads fly for up to 1 hour searching for schools of anchovy and travel up to 60km from colonies (flight speed 40–50km/h). Breeds colonially on cliffs and offshore islands; lays 1–5 eggs in a nest of vegetation, bones and feathers built on the ground, or on man-made structures. Eats pelagic fish (mainly anchovy and juv pelagic gobies) and benthic fish on the seabed to depth of 37m (dives lasting up to 1.3 minutes). Pelagic dives mainly 5–10m deep, lasting 20–30 seconds; descend less steeply than during benthic dives. Unusual among cormorants in roosting on the water during the day. Forages up to 80km offshore on the Agulhas Bank, and also feeds in coastal wetlands. Trekduiker

Br ad has more glossy plumage than Bank Cormorant

Br ad is much darker than juv (inset)

Br ad (top) has orange gular pouch, absent in juv (above)

Bank Cormorant *Phalacrocorax neglectus*   74–76cm; 1.6–2.3kg

A heavily built blackish cormorant confined to the Benguela coast from central Namibia to Cape Agulhas. Exclusively marine. Slightly larger but substantially heavier than Cape Cormorant; best told apart by its angled head profile resulting from its steep forehead and flat crown; feeds and commutes singly (not in flocks). Pre-br ad has a white rump patch. Partial leucism is fairly common, especially in the wings and tail. Eyes brown in fledglings, but soon turn turquoise, and then gradually brick-red, starting at the top of the eye and progressing down the eye with age; become almost entirely red in old birds. Juv slightly browner, but never as pale brown as juv Cape Cormorant. **Voice:** Wheezy '*wheee*' at colony; silent at sea. **Status and biology: ENDANGERED.** Endemic to the Benguela; only 3,000 pairs (9,000 pairs 30 years ago); reasons for decline unclear, but probably include disturbance, climate change and reduction in rock lobster numbers; population stable on south coast where lobsters are increasing. Most breed on Mercury Island, Namibia; South African population <500 pairs. Breeds colonially on offshore rocks and islands; most colonies small (5–50 pairs). Lays 1–3 eggs in nest built from fresh seaweed, plastered onto rock with guano. Foraging bouts typically last 25–80 minutes, comprising 5–20 dives. Br males have longer bouts than females. Seldom travels more than 20km from colonies; br ads return repeatedly to the same foraging area. Hunts on the seabed, diving to 50m; dives average about 70 seconds (max 2 minutes), with 30–60 seconds on the seabed. Eats a variety of fish, rock lobster, octopus and other marine invertebrates. Diet differs among colonies; ad pelagic gobies dominate the diet at Mercury Island. Bankduiker

Ad with aberrant white tail feathers

Imm in flight (top); ad feeding in a kelp bed (above)

Juv's turquoise eyes (top) gradually turn orange in ad (above)

137

White-breasted Cormorant *Phalacrocorax lucidus*   85–95cm; 1.7–3.2kg

The largest African cormorant; often treated as a subspecies of the widespread Great Cormorant *P. carbo*. Readily told from other cormorants by its large size, heavy build and extensive white underparts. Ad has white throat and breast, often washed pink in marine populations, possibly due to staining from seaweeds. Bare yellow skin on face and at base of bill, but gular pouch mostly feathered; eyes turquoise. Br ads have white thigh patches and fine white filoplumes on the head. Imm has white underparts (including the undertail coverts); upperparts browner. Juv has brown mottled breast and blackish undertail coverts; rest of underparts off-white; eyes pale brown. **Voice:** Grunts and squeaks at colony; otherwise silent. **Status and biology:** Some 100,000–200,000 pairs distributed locally throughout Africa. Fairly common resident at dams, lakes, large rivers, estuaries and shallow coastal waters. Ringing recoveries show that fledglings from inland sites visit the coast and vice versa. Breeds colonially; lays 3 or 4 (rarely 2 or 5) eggs in stick nests built in trees, bushes, reeds, on cliffs or on the ground on islands; sometimes associated with herons, ibises, egrets, darters or other cormorants. Forages mainly over sandy bottoms, swimming swiftly underwater at up to 4m/s. Foraging bouts at sea last up to 80 minutes.

Eats mainly fish, but opportunistic – steals prey from other cormorants and darters, and eats Cape Cormorant chicks on Namibian guano platforms. Dives to 33m (2.5 minutes), but usually dives much shallower; dive duration strongly linked to water depth; averages 20–30 seconds when diving in shallow water <3m deep. Witborsduiker

Imm has white underparts

Some ads have blackish breasts

Ad with white thigh patch and stained breast

Juv with dusky face and throat and whitish belly

Crozet Shag *Leucocarbo melanogenis*

70–75cm; 1.8–2.5kg

A striking, black-and-white cormorant confined to inshore waters around the Prince Edward and Crozet islands. Ad black above, glossed purple on body and greenish on wings, contrasting with white underparts and wing bar. Golden caruncles at base of bill, fleshy blue eye-ring, forecrown crest and pink feet all more prominent and brightly coloured at the start of the br season. Juv much duller; lacks facial ornaments; eye-ring grey; grey-brown upperparts merge into white underparts. **Voice:** Nasal, crow-like honk at colonies; usually silent at sea. **Status and biology:** Treated as a subspecies of Imperial Cormorant *L. atriceps* by BirdLife International;

1,000–2,000 pairs globally; CRITICALLY ENDANGERED in South Africa because the small population at the Prince Edward Islands (230–700 pairs) has decreased over the last few decades, although there are large fluctuations in numbers breeding each year. Breeds in small colonies on rock stacks and cliffs; mostly in summer, but breeding season is protracted, and sometimes breeds in winter; lays 2 or 3 (rarely 1 or up to 5) eggs. Feeds on bottom; seldom more than 1km from shore. Dives to 145m (6 minutes), but very long, deep dives use anaerobic respiration, requiring much longer recovery time between dives. Eats fish, octopus and crustaceans. Curious of ships; flies over to inspect them, and sometimes lands on the water nearby. Crozetduiker

Even non-br ads have yellow caruncles

Note the white lines on the upperwing

Non-br ad has striking black-and-white plumage

Juvs are duller than ads, with brownish upperparts

Crowned Cormorant *Microcarbo coronatus* 54–58cm; 680–860g

A small, short-billed and long-tailed marine cormorant confined to the west and south coasts. Closely related to Reed Cormorant, but is slightly larger, with a shorter, less graduated tail; ranges overlap narrowly in coastal wetlands; told apart with difficulty. Ad glossy black with prominent forecrown crest; back feathers less contrasting than in ad Reed Cormorant, with narrower black tips; appears more uniform from a distance. Eyes red. Facial skin and lower mandible orange, but face pink and swollen in pre-br birds. Juv slightly browner with paler throat and breast; crest smaller than ad's; eyes grey-brown; face and bill base dull orange-brown. Imm paler brown with whitish throat and breast, but lacks the extensive white underparts of imm Reed Cormorant; eyes dull red. **Voice:** Cackles and hisses at colony. **Status and biology:** Endemic br resident. NEAR THREATENED. 3,100 pairs breed colonially on cliffs and offshore islands from central Namibia to Cape Agulhas, although range extending eastwards – 12 pairs discovered breeding at Tsitsikamma in 2003. Largely resident, but juvs disperse up to 500km. Breeds in small colonies; lays 2 or 3 eggs (rarely 1 or up to 5) in a platform nest of vegetation, bones and feathers, built on bushes, rock outcrops or man-made structures; on some islands repeated use of the same sites has built up large stick towers supporting multiple nests. Occurs in coastal waters, sometimes roosting in nearby wetlands; seldom ventures offshore, but occasionally seen up to 10km from the coast. Eats fish, especially klipfish, and invertebrates. Forages on seabed, diving to 20m (max 1 minute), but mostly <5m. Kuifkopduiker

Non-br ad is darker below than Reed Cormorant

Br ad with its long crest erect

Juv (top) is dull brown; non-br ad (above) has pale throat

Reed Cormorant *Microcarbo africanus*

50–56cm; 440–650g

A small, short-billed and long-tailed cormorant found mainly in freshwater habitats. Range overlaps narrowly with that of Crowned Cormorant at coastal wetlands, but it is slightly smaller with a longer, more graduated tail. Ad glossy black with prominent forecrown crest; back feathers more contrasting than in ad Crowned Cormorant, with silver bases and broad black tips. Eyes red; facial skin orange. Non-br ad duller above with off-white underparts; moulting birds appear mottled below. Juv brown with slightly paler underparts and brown eyes. Imm whitish below with red-brown eyes. **Voice:** Cackles and hisses at colony. **Status and biology:** Some 100,000–200,000 pairs breed throughout sub-Saharan Africa. Locally common resident at dams, lakes, rivers and estuaries. Avoids marine habitats in most of sthn Africa (e.g. commuting between wetlands over parts of False Bay without landing) but exploits shallow coastal waters in Mozambique and N Namibia. Breeds colonially, laying 3 or 4 (up to 6) eggs in stick or reed nests in trees, bushes, reeds, cliffs or on the ground on islands; often associated with herons, ibises, egrets, darters or other cormorants. Eats small fish, frogs, crabs and other invertebrates; often feeds in groups, sometimes with Cape Cormorants. Feeds mainly in shallow water <2m, but to depth of 10m; max dive duration 45 seconds. Travels slowly underwater (1–2m/s). Foraging bouts average 20 minutes, but occasionally up to 84 minutes. Recovers body temperature after a long bout by sitting with its wings spread and back to the sun. **Rietduiker**

Imm has mostly white underparts

Br ad has strongly contrasting back feathers

Swimming birds sit low in the water

Non-br ad moulting into br plumage

141

Female Red (Grey) Phalarope on its breeding grounds; the birds seldom attain this plumage in sthn Africa

PHALAROPES

The phalaropes are a small genus of shorebirds in the family Scolopacidae. All 3 species are long-distance migrants that breed in the northern hemisphere and winter mainly south of the equator, but only 2 qualify as seabirds; Wilson's Phalarope has poorly developed salt glands and seldom occurs at sea. The 2 marine species both have circumpolar breeding distributions in the northern tundra. Red Phalaropes breed farther north, and mostly migrate farther south than Red-necked Phalaropes, and so are the ones most often found at sea off southern Africa.

Like storm petrels, phalaropes appear out of place at sea. They are usually seen flying swiftly, low over the water, resembling Sanderlings. They feed by picking small prey items from the sea surface, and enhance prey encounter rates by feeding at drift lines where surface waters converge, concentrating floating items. They also use their lobed toes to swim in tight circles,

spinning at 40–60 revolutions per minute, to create a vortex that draws zooplankton to the surface from as much as 0.5m below the surface.

Females are the dominant sex, larger and more brightly coloured than males. They are polyandrous; females mate with multiple males, leaving each with a clutch of 3 or 4 eggs. The precocial chicks are brooded by the male, but feed themselves. Adults undergo a complete post-breeding moult that starts on the breeding grounds, is suspended during migration, and completed on the wintering grounds. They acquire their distinctive breeding plumage in a partial pre-breeding moult starting at the end of March.

Although neither species is threatened globally, like many long-distance migrants their numbers are decreasing. Their habit of feeding along drift lines predisposes them to eat floating debris, and both species often ingest plastic fragments.

Red (Grey) Phalarope *Phalaropus fulicarius*

20–22cm; 40–68g

The common phalarope at sea off sthn Africa. Larger and paler than Red-necked Phalarope, with a shorter, thicker bill that is broad to the tip and may show a yellow base. Head mainly white with black eye patch. Hind neck, back and rump are rather plain grey, but can look mottled in moulting birds. In br plumage (rarely recorded in sthn Africa) has chestnut underparts and white face. Juv browner above; breast tinged buffy. **Voice:** Soft, low *'wiit'*. **Status and biology:** Up to 500,000 pairs breed in the far northern tundra; winter in the S Humboldt, Benguela and Canary upwelling regions. Fairly common off the west coast, uncommon in the Agulhas Current to 40°S, and rare off the east coast; vagrants occur along the coast and on inland lakes. Usually found in small flocks at sea. Eats mainly zooplankton. Forages along drift lines or by spinning in calm weather to pull prey to the surface. Grysfraiingpoot

Non-br ad has plain grey back; note broad bill

In flight, rump is grey (not blackish)

Red-necked Phalarope *Phalaropus lobatus*

17–20cm; 28–45g

Slightly smaller than Red Phalarope, with a darker grey back streaked with white, and a longer, thinner, all-black bill (lacking a yellow base). In flight, appears darker above with a blackish (not grey) rump. Body is dark grey in br plumage, with rufous neck band; female is more brightly coloured than male. Juv darker and browner above, with rufous-fringed feathers; breast washed buff. **Voice:** Low *'tchick'* in flight. **Status and biology:** Up to 1 million pairs breed in the northern tundra; winters in the northern Humboldt Current, Arabian Sea and South China Sea; not recorded at sea off sthn Africa (although perhaps overlooked among more common Red Phalaropes). Regular in small numbers at saltpans at Walvis Bay and Berg River estuary; rare at other wetlands. Eats small insects and crustaceans. Rooihalsfraiingpoot

Non-br ad has needle-like bill

Some overwintering birds acquire br plumage: female (left) and male (right)

143

Ad Brown Skuas defend a brood of newly hatched chicks on Inaccessible Island

SKUAS AND JAEGERS

The skuas and jaegers (Stercorariidae) are predatory, gull-like birds that are unique in having sharp, curved claws combined with webbed toes. The 4 larger skuas have been moved back into *Catharacta*, separate from the 3 smaller jaegers, despite the evolution of Pomarine Jaeger from hybrids between Parasitic Jaegers and Great skuas *C. skua* from the N Atlantic. Taxonomy of *Catharacta* skuas is messy, with ongoing gene flow among at least some species. Brown and South Polar Skuas regularly hybridise where their breeding ranges overlap on the Antarctic Peninsula; a ringed

hybrid chick photographed off South Africa was indistinguishable from a Brown Skua.

All species breed at high to mid-latitudes, with 4 species in the northern and 3 in the southern hemisphere. Almost all birds leave their breeding grounds to winter at sea. The 3 jaegers are trans-Equatorial migrants, whereas among *Catharacta*, only South Polar Skuas regularly winter in the opposite hemisphere. Recent tracking studies have provided fascinating insights into the migration routes of these birds, which differ among species and with breeding location. For example, South Polar Skuas breeding at the world's largest Antarctic

Imm Pomarine Jaegers harassing a Black-legged Kittiwake in the Arctic

Petrel colony at Svarthamaren, south of Africa, winter in the Indian Ocean, whereas those from farther east along the Antarctic coast, south of Australia, winter in both the Indian and North Pacific, and those from the Antarctic Peninsula winter in both the North Atlantic and North Pacific, with a few remaining in the southern hemisphere (Humboldt Current and around Tristan/Gough). By comparison, Brown Skuas breeding at the Crozet and Kerguelen archipelagos show much greater individual variation in wintering areas. Most individuals favour fairly small areas across a vast expanse of the southern Indian Ocean, but others disperse more widely, reaching the coast of South Africa and Namibia, the Seychelles, Indonesia and Western and South Australia.

Brown Skua eggs pipping

Like gulls, skuas are versatile predators. They are renowned for stealing food from other birds (kleptoparasitism). This behaviour is best developed in Parasitic Jaegers, which are professional pirates that obtain much of their food by harrying other birds. However, most skuas are largely predatory when breeding and often scavenge food when not. Breeding adults are extremely adaptable, with pairs specialising in different prey types in relation to local availability in space (e.g. penguins vs petrels at sub-Antarctic islands) and time (e.g. lemmings in the Arctic tundra). They are extremely intelligent predators, and pairs work together to steal eggs or chicks from breeding penguins. At Marion Island, a single pair of Brown Skuas can cause almost complete breeding failure at a small colony of Macaroni Penguins.

Females average larger than males, but the difference is often subtle. South Polar Skuas are more sexually dimorphic than Brown Skuas and show greater segregation in breeding roles. Plumage varies with age and among individuals. Adding to the complexity, the jaegers and South Polar Skuas have pale, intermediate and dark morphs. All undergo a complete post-breeding moult and a partial pre-breeding moult, resulting in distinct non-breeding and breeding plumages in the jaegers, but little seasonal plumage difference in the skuas. All species take up to 3 years to acquire adult plumage.

Most adults are monogamous, but a few Brown Skuas form polyandrous trios. All are highly territorial; adults that are unable to obtain sites await breeding opportunities in non-breeding 'clubs'. They lay 1 or 2 well-camouflaged eggs in a shallow scrape on the ground. Both sexes incubate and feed the semi-precocial chicks, which continue to be fed for several weeks after fledging.

No species is globally threatened, but the Subantarctic Skua, which belongs to the Brown Skua complex, is listed as Endangered in South Africa. Their numbers at Marion Island were expected to increase once cats were eradicated, as these birds as well as the cats eat burrowing petrels. However, the number of skua pairs has decreased over the last 30 years, while the Prince Edward Island population is stable. The reason for their decrease on Marion may be linked to decreases in penguin populations.

Gulls and terns use their faster turning ability to elude chasing skuas

Long-tailed Jaeger *Stercorarius longicaudus* 38cm (to 62cm with streamers); 230–420g

The smallest jaeger, with buoyant, tern-like flight on long, slender wings. Bill short; at close range, nail (upper mandible tip) comprises roughly half bill length (less than a third in Parasitic Jaeger). Almost all ads are pale morphs: plain, cold greyish above, with only the shafts of outer 2 primaries white; vent and uppertail coverts barred in non-br plumage. Very long central tail feathers are diagnostic in br plumage, but streamers shorter when moulting or broken. Juv varies from pale to dark brown; usually colder grey-brown above than juv Parasitic Jaeger, with more boldly barred uppertail coverts, underwing, vent and flanks (but underwing rather

uniform dark brown in very dark individuals). Imms are less variable than juvs, converging on pale grey-brown ad plumage. **Voice:** Silent at sea. **Status and biology:** 50,000 pairs breed in the Arctic tundra in the northern summer; winter in oceanic waters of the southern hemisphere to 50°S. Migrates with Arctic Terns and, to a lesser extent, Sabine's Gulls. Although only discovered off sthn Africa in the 1970s, it is fairly common in the region, travelling in flocks of up to 30 birds. Often loosely associated with groups of Arctic Terns. Scarce close to land, but occasionally pushed inshore by strong winds during passage; vagrant inland. Diet in the region poorly known; occasionally scavenges at trawlers; seldom harries other seabirds. **Langstertroofmeeu**

Juv with heavily barred uppertail coverts

Non-br Long-tailed Jaeger in moult

Top to bottom: br ad, imm, non-br ad

Parasitic Jaeger *Stercorarius parasiticus*   46cm (to 65cm with streamers); 320–600g

A medium-sized jaeger with white wing flashes; usually the most abundant jaeger in coastal waters off sthn Africa. Larger and somewhat more heavily built than Long-tailed Jaeger, with broader wings and more prominent white wing flashes; flight more direct and dashing. Plumage generally darker brown (not pale grey-brown). More likely to be confused with Pomarine Jaeger (p.148), but is smaller and more slender, with relatively longer, narrower wings that have longer 'hands' and shorter 'arms'; bill distinctly smaller and appears uniformly dark; pale-phase birds have a smaller dark hood and a paler yellow neck patch. If present, central tail feathers are relatively short and straight. Pale, dark and rare intermediate colour morphs occur. Juv more rusty brown than other juv jaegers, with less strongly barred underparts. Imm and non-br ads have barred flanks, rumps and undertail coverts. **Voice:** Silent at sea. **Status and biology:** 100,000 pairs breed in the Arctic tundra in the northern summer; winter mainly in southern hemisphere. Individuals tend to winter in the same area in successive years, but do not follow the usual leap-frog migration pattern; birds from Svalbard winter off N and W Africa, whereas those from Norway and Scotland reach the Benguela and the Patagonian Shelf. Fairly common migrant to coastal waters, but scarce off the east coast; rare in oceanic waters. Vagrant inland, but occasionally roosts ashore, especially in N Namibia. Most occur Oct–Apr, but small numbers overwinter. Steals food from terns and gulls; rarely kills storm petrels; also scavenges at fishing vessels. Arktiese Roofmeeu

Ad on breeding grounds

Dark morph ad in moult

Juv with barred flanks and vent, and short tail streamers

Imm in moult

Ad in breeding plumage

147

Pomarine Jaeger *Stercorarius pomarinus*   50cm (to 75cm with streamers); 550–900g

A large, heavily built jaeger. Its mitochondrial DNA is very similar to that of the Great Skua *S. skua* – either Great Skua is a hybrid between female Pomarine Jaegers and one of the southern skuas, or (more likely) Pomarine Jaeger is a hybrid between female Great Skuas and a jaeger. Best told from Parasitic Jaeger (p.147) by its heavy barrel-chest, stout, pale-based bill, and broad wings with large white wing flashes; rump and tail appear shorter than in other jaegers. It is so large and heavily built that it can be confused with a South Polar Skua (p.150). Flight direct and powerful. Br ad has spoon-shaped central tail feathers. Pale morphs predominate; have a more extensive dark cap, darker yellow neck patch and often a bolder breast band than other pale-morph jaegers. Non-br ads are barred on vent, flanks and rump. Juvs and imms are boldly barred on belly, vent, rump and underwing; distinguished from other jaegers at all ages by their two-tone bill. **Voice:** Silent at sea. **Status and biology:** 20,000 pairs breed in the Arctic tundra in the northern summer, where heavily dependent on lemmings. Ads are nomadic, breeding where lemmings are abundant, and seldom retain the same mate in successive years. Spends the northern winter in tropical and south-temperate seas, mainly in coastal waters. Fairly common along the west coast, especially in Namibia, from Oct–Apr; scarce off the east coast, and rare in oceanic waters. Occasionally roosts ashore in N Namibia. Steals food from gannets, terns and other seabirds; also scavenges at fishing vessels. **Knopstertroofmeeu**

Br ad pale phase

Ad starting post-br moult

ADAM RILEY

Non-br ad from above

Imm showing barred axillaries

Note broad-based wings and short 'hand'

JOHN GRAHAM

148

Brown (Subantarctic) Skua *Catharacta antarctica* 56–66cm; 1.3–2.1kg

A large, heavy-bodied skua with large, white wing flashes. Short, broad wings, short rump and tail, and heavy build distinguish it from jaegers. Upperparts are variably streaked and blotched buff; plainer in juvs and imms, which also have less extensive white wing flashes. Larger, chunkier and heavier-billed than South Polar (p.150) and Chilean (p.151) skuas; underwing coverts brown (not blackish or rufous). **Voice:** Display at colonies is a loud '*aah aah-aah-ah-ah-ah-ah-ah*' with wings raised; generally silent at sea. **Status and biology:** Not threatened globally, but **ENDANGERED** in South Africa due to recent decreases at Marion Island. 12,000 pairs breed around the Southern Ocean in summer – 1,200 pairs of Tristan Skuas *S. a. hamiltoni* at Tristan da Cunha and Gough Island, 1,000 pairs of Subantarctic Skuas *S. a. lonnbergi* at the Prince Edward Islands. Races are not monophyletic (at least for mitochondrial DNA), and even some South Polar and Chilean skua lineages are interspersed among the Brown Skua complex. Female Subantarctic Skuas hybridise with South Polar Skuas in the Antarctic Peninsula; ringed hybrids recorded off South Africa. Subantarctic

Skuas are common in shelf waters; most are from the Prince Edward Islands and probably the Crozets, although some from Kerguelen and S Georgia (but not the S Sandwiches) also winter off sthn Africa; presence of Tristan Skuas not confirmed. Lays 1 or 2 eggs in a shallow cup nest on the ground. Breeding birds eat mainly burrowing petrels or penguin eggs and chicks. Wintering birds scavenge at sea; regularly attend trawlers; only occasionally steal food from gannets and shearwaters. Bruinroofmeeu

Ad displaying dark brown underwing coverts

Ad and juv (inset) Tristan Skua *S. a. hamiltoni*

Brown underwing coverts can appear blackish; sits high on the water (inset)

South Polar Skua *Catharacta maccormicki* 52–58cm; 1.1–1.5kg

Smaller and more slender than Brown Skua (p.149); body shape can recall Pomarine Jaeger (p.148). Head and breast vary from dark brown (dark morph) to ash (pale morph). Plumage rather plain, with only fine, sparse streaks on neck and back. Pale morph is easily identified by contrast between dark wings and pale head and body. Dark morph resembles a slender juv Brown Skua with a small bill; often has paler, greyish feathers at base of bill; blackish underwing coverts diagnostic. Intermediate birds usually show a pale hind neck, also shown by many Subantarctic Skuas. Juv plain brown, lacking paler face or nape. Sits more upright on water than other large skuas. **Voice:** Similar to that of Brown Skua. **Status and biology:** Some 6,000 pairs breed at ice-free areas in Antarctica in summer. Most migrate to the northern hemisphere in winter. Individuals visit the same wintering area each year, but birds from the same colony disperse widely. Rare in sthn Africa, mainly on passage, but some ads from Queen Maud Land winter in the Mozambique Channel. Opportunistic kleptoparasite and predator; often pugnacious, even tackling albatrosses. Suidpoolroofmeeu

Displaying ad showing blackish underwing coverts

Pale ad sitting on water

Darker birds resemble Brown Skua

Intermediate morphs often show a pale collar

Extent of white wing flashes vary

Chilean Skua *Catharacta chilensis*

53–59cm; 1.2–1.5kg

Smaller than Brown Skua (p.149); structure recalls South Polar Skua, but has rufous (not blackish) underwing coverts; underparts mottled or entirely rufous. Ad usually has a dark cap; bill base paler grey than tip. Juv more uniformly coloured than ad, with rich cinnamon underparts. **Voice:** Similar to that of Brown Skua. **Status and biology:** Several thousand pairs breed in Patagonia and S Chile in summer. Vagrant; one record from Inaccessible Island, Tristan da Cunha, loosely associated with a club of non-br Tristan Skuas in Nov 2009, and another on Marion Island in a club of Subantarctic Skuas in Nov 2017. Opportunistic kleptoparasite and predator. Chileroofmeeu

Displaying ad showing rufous underwing coverts

Ad showing dark cap and cinnamon belly

Juv is more rufous than ad

Ads often show a paler collar

Ad is less distinctive from above

151

Kelp Gulls soar over their breeding colony

GULLS

The gulls were formerly placed in their own family, but we now know that the noddies and fairy terns are an ancestral lineage, basal to the gulls, skimmers and other terns, so they have all been combined into a single family, Laridae. The gulls are treated separately here for convenience. Gull taxonomy also is in a state of flux, with some 50–60 species recognised, divided into 10 genera. They occur on all continents, but are most diverse in the northern hemisphere. They range in size from the Little Gull (125g) to the Great Black-backed Gull (1.85kg). Species limits among *Larus* gulls remain controversial, with localised hybridisation among some populations.

Gulls are among the most versatile of seabirds. Although a few species are exclusively marine (e.g. kittiwakes), many species are equally at home on land, at sea and in freshwater habitats. They owe much of their success to their extremely adaptable foraging behaviour. Supreme generalists, they forage by surface picking or shallow diving, as well as by taking food while on land or in the air. They steal food from other birds, scavenge scraps from predators, and are open to explore new potential food resources. Recently, Kelp Gulls have caused concern by pecking blubber from Southern Right Whales. Gulls generally cope well in human-altered habitats, taking advantage of novel food sources. For example, Hartlaub's Gulls feed on earthworms after heavy rains flood sports fields, and Kelp Gulls eat introduced Mediterranean Snails *Theba pisana* in west coast fields. Both species have expanded their ranges inland thanks to human land-use changes. Many gulls scavenge scraps at rubbish dumps, but they tend to revert to a natural, higher-quality diet when raising chicks.

The sexes look alike, but males average slightly larger than females. Most species undergo a complete post-breeding moult and a partial pre-breeding moult, resulting in distinct non-breeding and breeding plumages. Franklin's Gull is atypical in having two complete moults each year. Juvenile body plumage is replaced within a few months of fledging, and thus unlikely to be observed in southern Africa for migrant and vagrant species. Small gulls attain adult-like plumage after 1–2 years, but large gulls take up to 4 years to acquire full adult plumage. Among immatures, the colour of new feathers depends in part on hormone levels when they are grown, resulting in a confusing array of plumages even among birds of the same age.

Most gulls are monogamous, and retain the same mate in successive years. The pair bond is reinforced by courtship feeding. Lesbian pairs are fairly common in some species, particularly where their ranges are expanding and males – which disperse less than females – are in short supply. However, some pesticides can also skew sex ratios towards females, promoting the formation of lesbian pairs. Trios – usually one male and two females – also occur sporadically.

All gulls are colonial breeders, and most species aggressively mob intruders, shrieking at and even striking them. Gulls nest in a wide range of habitats, from islands and cliffs to wetlands, reedbeds and the roofs of buildings. Nest structures are equally varied, ranging from a shallow scrape on the ground to a large bowl of vegetation. They lay 1–3 well-camouflaged eggs; larger clutches of up to 6 eggs probably result from more than one female laying in the same nest. A replacement clutch is often laid if the first clutch is lost. Both sexes incubate and feed the semi-precocial chicks, which are fed for several weeks after fledging (and which continue to beg for even longer).

The adaptability of gulls makes them the least threatened large group of seabirds; of the 50 species recognised by the IUCN, only 6 are globally threatened and 4 are Near Threatened. Of the southern African species, only the vagrant Black-legged Kittiwake is Vulnerable; Hartlaub's Gull is listed as Vulnerable in Namibia.

Gull chicks, like these Kelp Gulls, are semi-precocial

Gulls are versatile foragers, taking a wide range of prey; this Kelp Gull is eating a kelp fly

Kelp Gull *Larus dominicanus* 55–65cm; 800–1,200g

The largest gull in the region; more heavily built than Lesser Black-backed Gull (p.156), with shorter wings and a more robust bill. Ad has blackish back and upperwings; eyes in ad *L. d. vetula* dark grey-brown (rarely yellow or silver-grey); legs olive-grey (rarely yellowish). Juv heavily streaked dark brown; bill blackish; legs brownish-pink. Best told from juv Lesser Black-backed Gull by structure; could potentially be confused with large skuas, but lacks neat white primary bases, and bill has typical gull shape. Takes 4 years to acquire full ad plumage; second-year birds have white body with diffuse brown smudging; mantle slate-grey with some brown feathers; tail tip blackish; bill pinkish at base and tip. Third-years have mostly ad plumage but typically retain some brown in upper- and underwings and outer tail; bill usually has a dark subterminal mark. **Voice:** Display call is long series of 'kee-ah' notes; alarm calls include single 'kee-ah', 'kwok' and 'yap-yap'. **Status and biology:** Widespread in southern hemisphere; 20,000 pairs of the endemic race *L. d. vetula* breed from S Angola to E Cape. Common resident in coastal habitats; follows trawlers up to 100km from shore, and increasingly found in agricultural lands up to 50km inland. Nominate *L. d. dominicanus* is regular vagrant from S America to Tristan da Cunha/Gough Island and possibly sthn Africa. Smaller *L. d. judithae* is resident at sub-Antarctic islands in the Indian Ocean, with 130 pairs at the Prince Edward Islands. Breeds in summer; lays 2 or 3 (rarely 1 or up to 5) eggs in a shallow scrape. Opportunistic scavenger and predator, taking wide range of prey, including mussels, limpets, snails, other invertebrates, fish, squid, small mammals, and birds' eggs and chicks.
Kelpmeeu

Br ad (top), second winter (centre) and juv (above)

Subantarctic Kelp Gull *L. d. judithae* br ad

Subantarctic Kelp Gull *L. d. judithae* third winter

Kelp Gull *L. d. vetula* br ad

Kelp Gull *L. d. vetula* third winter

Kelp Gull *L. d. vetula* second winter

Kelp Gull *L. d. vetula* first winter

Lesser Black-backed Gull *Larus fuscus* 52–65cm; 560–1,150g

Slightly smaller than Kelp Gull (p.154), with a less robust bill and more attenuated appearance; wings project well beyond the tail at rest. Head less robust, with gently sloping forehead. Several races occur, sometimes treated as separate species: 'Baltic Gull' *L. f. fuscus* (breeds from Denmark to the White Sea in Russia) is smaller (560–800g), with a blackish-grey back in ad plumage; 'Heuglin's Gull' *L. f. heuglini* (breeds in central Siberia from the Kola Peninsula to the Taimyr Peninsula) is larger (850–1,150g), with a longer bill and shallow forehead, giving it a rakish appearance; ad back slate-grey, becoming paler grey at the eastern edge of the range; 'Steppe Gull' *L. f. barabensis* (central Asia) is intermediate in size, with an even paler grey back. Ads have yellow legs and feet (not olive-grey like most Kelp Gulls). Juvs and imms best differentiated by structure; legs are typically paler, flesh-coloured (not brownish), but note large variation among Kelp Gulls in both structure and leg colour.

Voice: Typical, large-gull '*kow-kow*'; shorter '*kop*'.

Status and biology: At least 300,000 pairs breed from Iceland and NW Europe to Siberia; most winter in the northern hemisphere, but small numbers from the eastern part of its range cross the equator, reaching sthn Africa. Most records are imms of the nominate race; status of Heuglin's and Steppe gulls uncertain. Often recorded from inland wetlands, but possibly overlooked at coastal sites; regular in small numbers in coastal Mozambique, mainly Oct–Apr; some imm birds overwinter. Omnivorous; an opportunistic forager similar to the Kelp Gull. Kleinswartrugmeeu

Lesser Black-backed Gull third winter

Second winter

Second summer

First winter

Non-br ad *L. f. fuscus*

Non-br ad *L. f. heuglini*

Non-br ad *L. f. barabensis*

First winter *L. f. barabensis*

Third winter *L. f. barabensis*

L. f. barabensis second winter (top) and ad winter (above)

Grey-headed Gull *Chroicocephalus cirrocephalus*   40–42cm; 250–350g

A medium-sized gull with a pale grey back and upperwings; superficially similar to Hartlaub's Gull. Ads' eyes are silver with narrow red outer ring. Br ad has a diagnostic pale grey head, and red bill and legs. Non-br ad has largely white head with grey smudges above eye and on cheeks; bill and legs usually duller. Imm has dark smudges on ear coverts and a dark-tipped, pink-orange bill. Juv is heavily mottled brown on upperwings; secondaries darker grey than in ad. Larger than Hartlaub's Gull, with a longer bill, slightly drooped at the tip. Easily told from vagrant gulls in flight by grey underwing and mostly black outer primaries. **Voice:** Dry '*karrh*'. **Status and biology:** At least 20,000 pairs breed locally in sub-Saharan Africa, Madagascar and S America (Ecuador–Peru and Brazil–Argentina), with at least 2,000 pairs in sthn Africa. Breeds in colonies at wetlands; lays 1–3 eggs in a shallow bowl of vegetation. Occasionally hybridises with Hartlaub's Gull; fate of offspring not known. Resident in some areas, but nomadic in others, breeding sporadically when conditions are favourable in Botswana and Namibia. Ringing recoveries show that juvs from Gauteng disperse widely throughout sthn Africa and to Angola and Zambia. An opportunistic scavenger and predator; feeds mainly in aquatic habitats, but also around towns and in agricultural lands. **Gryskopmeeu**

Br ad showing pale grey head and grey underwings

Non-br ad in moult; note pale eye and grey head smudges

Br ad

Juv has black tail bar

Imm with dark-tipped bill

Hartlaub's Gull *Chroicocephalus hartlaubii*

38–40cm; 230–340g

Slightly smaller than Grey-headed Gull, with a shorter, thinner and darker bill and deeper red legs; eyes usually dark at all ages. Told from vagrant gulls in flight by grey underwing and mostly black outer primaries (although aberrant individuals have mainly white outer primaries). Br ads have slight lavender shadow 'hood'; non-br birds have plain white head. Imm has uniform dark bill and dull legs; sometimes shows small dark patches on ear coverts. Juv is mottled brown on wing coverts, but is less heavily mottled than juv Grey-headed Gull. **Voice:** Drawn-out, rattling *'keeerrh'*. **Status and biology:** Endemic to Benguela Upwelling region. Common resident; 8,000–12,000 pairs breed on offshore islands, large buildings at the coast and at coastal wetlands up to 30km inland from central Namibia to Gqeberha, E Cape; breeding range has extended eastward along the south coast in the last decade. Not threatened globally, but **VULNERABLE** in Namibia due to poor breeding success linked to disturbance and introduced predators at colonies. Occasionally hybridises with Grey-headed Gulls. Lays 1–3 eggs in a shallow bowl of vegetation. Opportunistic scavenger and predator, mainly in coastal habitats, but also around towns and on flooded fields. Often active at night; takes insects attracted to lights, and birds returning to colonies from offshore in the early morning suggest that they also feed nocturnally at sea. Hartlaubmeeu

Br ad showing grey underwing

Br ad (top) and juv moulting into imm plumage (above)

Upperwing patterns of br ad and juv (inset)

Slender-billed Gull *Chroicocephalus genei*

38–44cm; 240–340g

A pale grey-and-white gull with a white head and distinctive head profile – shallow sloping forehead and long bill that droops slightly at the tip. Ad has pale eyes and red bill (duller when non-br); underparts washed pink in br plumage. In flight, wing pattern resembles Black-headed Gull's, but body appears longer. Imm has orange bill with dusky tip; dark smudge behind eye, but this is less prominent than in imm Grey-headed (p.158) and Black-headed gulls. **Voice:** '*Ka*' or '*kra*', deeper than Black-headed Gull. **Status and biology:** Some 100,000 pairs breed from Mauritania to India and central Asia; wintering in NE Africa. Rare vagrant to sthn Africa; only one record from Durban, Sept 1999. Eats fish and invertebrates. Dunbekmeeu

Br ad showing long bill and gently sloping forehead

Non-br ad (top), imm (middle) and br ad (above)

Imm Slender-billed Gull (left) and an ad Grey-headed Gull (right)

Black-headed Gull *Chroicocephalus ridibundus* 35–40cm; 200–320g

Paler grey above than Grey-headed (p.158) and Hartlaub's (p.159) gulls; in flight, has mostly white outer primaries (but aberrant Hartlaub's and Grey-headed can also show this) and whitish (not grey) underwings. Br ad has dark brown hood and partial white eye-ring; bill dark red. Non-br ads have dark smudges on head and paler red bill with dark tip. Imm similar but with dark brownish subterminal band across inner primaries, secondaries and tail. Juv has mottled brown wing coverts; unlikely to occur in this plumage in the region. **Voice:** Typical, small-gull '*kraah*'. **Status and biology:** Some 2 million pairs breed in Eurasia; winter south to Tanzania; vagrant to sthn Africa. Most records are with other gulls at coastal or inland wetlands. Omnivorous; eats mainly invertebrates. Swartkopmeeu

Br ad showing chocolate hood and narrow white eye-ring

Br ad showing whitish underwing coverts

Non-br ad showing extensive white in outer wing

Ad moulting into br plumage

Non-br ad in worn plumage

Franklin's Gull *Leucophaeus pipixcan*

32–36cm; 210–320g

A fairly small, black-headed gull with a rather short, stubby bill and at least partial black hood with white crescents above and below the eye at all ages. Darker grey above than other small gulls in the region, other than vagrant Laughing Gull. In flight, ad has broad white trailing edge to secondaries; black subterminal band on outer primaries surrounded by white. Underwings whitish. Bill dark red in br plumage; black in non-br and imm birds. Br ad often washed pink on underparts. First winter has darker grey wings than ad with dark grey outer primaries, but still has broad white trailing edge to secondaries and inner primaries; underparts white and tail white with a black subterminal band. **Voice:** Silent in Africa. **Status and biology:** Some 200,000–300,000 pairs breed at wetlands in the N American prairies; migrate south to winter in Central America and along the west coast of S America. Its salt glands regress when it lives in freshwater wetlands in summer, but start to enlarge before it reaches marine habitats. The only non-passerine that typically undergoes two complete moults each year. Starts the first moult on its breeding ground in Jul, and usually completes it before migrating in Oct. Second moult commences on wintering grounds in Dec, and continues slowly, with outer primaries still growing on arrival at breeding grounds. Vagrant to the coast and adjacent wetlands in sthn Africa, with a few records from inland waterbodies. Eats mainly small fish and invertebrates. **Franklinmeeu**

Br ad showing broad white trailing edge to wing

Br ad (top) and non-br ad (above)

Juv showing brown upperwing and black tail tip

Laughing Gull *Leucophaeus atricilla*

36–41cm; 230–400g

Similar to Franklin's Gull but slightly larger with a longer, more drooped bill and longer legs. Ad best told by mostly black primaries with at most small white tips; lacks the bold black and white primary tips of ad Franklin's Gull. Br ad has narrower white eye crescents than Franklin's Gull; non-br ad has less black on the head. First winter has blacker outer wing than Franklin's Gull, with a black tail (not subterminal black band), and grey wash on the sides of the breast and flanks. Second winter has mostly white tail and some grey wash on the flanks. **Voice:** Silent in Africa. **Status and biology:** Some 200,000 pairs breed at coastal wetlands along the east coast of the Americas from Maine to French Guiana, and locally in western Mexico; winters S along the coast to Peru and NE Brazil. Rare vagrant to sthn Africa; only one record from Mossel Bay in Feb 2022. Omnivorous; eats small fish, invertebrates and scraps. Roetvlerkmeeu

Br ad showing black wing tip

Br ad from below

Ad showing long, slightly drooped bill

Imm has grey-washed underparts

Imm has black wing tip like ad

163

Sooty Gull *Ichthyaetus hemprichii*

42–50cm; 400–510g

A mid-sized gull with dark grey-brown upperparts and a long and slightly drooped bill. Br ad has blackish hood contrasting with white hind neck collar and dark grey breast and flanks; belly white. Bill yellow with black and red tip; legs yellow. Non-br ad duller with grey-brown head. Imm has pale blue-grey bill with black tip. Upperwing and underwing dark grey-brown with a narrow white trailing edge at all ages. Unlikely to be confused with any gull in the region; most similar to smaller White-eyed Gull *I. leucopthalmus* from the Red Sea and Somalia, which has a darker, longer and more slender bill, paler grey back and more prominent white eye crescents at all ages. **Voice:** Various wailing and laughing calls, but generally silent when not breeding. **Status and biology:** Some 50,000 pairs breed from N Kenya to Pakistan. After breeding, disperses along coasts, including south to Tanzania. Vagrant to sthn Africa; probably all records of one individual initially recorded at St Lucia in Nov 2020, then spent several weeks at Kei Mouth before being seen in Algoa Bay into Apr 2021. Omnivorous; eats small fish, invertebrates, baby turtles and scraps. **Bruin Meeu**

Br ad; note dark upperwing and white tail

Non-br ad

Non-br ad has dark grey breast

Br and non-br ads sitting on water

Imm with subterminal black tail band

Sabine's Gull *Xema sabini*

27–32cm; 170–210g

A small, oceanic gull with a shallow-forked tail and buoyant, tern-like flight. In flight, boldly tricoloured upperwing is diagnostic. Ad bill black with yellow tip; legs black. Non-br ads have mostly white head with dark smudges on nape; br ads have dark grey hood. Juv upperparts brownish, scaled white; in flight, show darker upperwing coverts. Bill black; legs grey-pink. **Voice:** Silent in Africa. **Status and biology:** Some 100,000 pairs breed in the northern tundra, mainly in N America, with smaller numbers in Greenland, Svalbard and Siberia. Most winter in the Humboldt and Benguela Upwelling regions. Birds tracked from E Greenland stage off W Europe for 5–7 weeks from late Aug to mid-Oct, then travel south through the Gulf of Guinea to reach the Benguela by mid-Nov. They depart north again in Apr, travelling in a more direct route to the Canary Current between Senegal and Mauritania, where they remain for 2–3 weeks before heading back to their breeding sites. Common migrant to coastal waters off the west coast of sthn Africa, often in flocks. Favours large bays, but also occurs out to the shelf edge, where it visits fishing vessels. Roosts at sea; very rarely comes ashore or visits coastal wetlands. Eats fish, crustaceans and fishery wastes; also gathers at offshore sewage discharges. Mikstertmeeu

Non-br ad showing diagnostic tricoloured wing

Juv has brownish upperparts and a dark tail tip

Non-br ad in worn plumage (br ad has a slate grey hood)

Black-legged Kittiwake *Rissa tridactyla*

36–40cm; 320–500g

An oceanic gull, slightly larger than Sabine's Gull (p.165), with long wings, a shallow-forked tail and short bill. Br ad white with pale grey back; upperwing pale grey with narrow white trailing edge and black tips to outer primaries; bill yellow. Non-br ad has grey patch on ear coverts and grey smudging on hind neck. Juv has black 'M' across upperwing, black tail tip (broadest in centre of tail) and black hind collar; bill black. **Voice:** Usually silent at sea. **Status and biology:** VULNERABLE, despite being the most abundant gull in the world; some 4–5 million pairs breed at coastal cliffs and islands in the N Atlantic, N Pacific and Arctic oceans. Most winter in temperate waters of the N Atlantic and N Pacific oceans; seldom crosses the equator. At best a rare vagrant to sthn Africa; 3 records claimed from the west coast, but no photographs or specimens so status in the region requires confirmation. Eats small fish and invertebrates. Swartpootbrandervoël

Non-br ad in moult

First summer showing under- (top) and upperwing (above)

First winter at sea

Juv showing distinctive black collar

Antarctic Terns roosting on Malgas Island

TERNS

Terns are more slender and elegant than gulls, with light, buoyant flight. They were previously placed in their own family, Sternidae, but genetic evidence shows that the noddies and white terns are an ancestral lineage, basal to the gulls, skimmers and other terns, so they are now all classified in a single large family, Laridae. The 47 or so species include 5 noddies in one genus, the White Tern complex, and 41 'typical' terns in 9 genera. Terns are found throughout the world, and are generally smaller than gulls, ranging in size from the Least Tern (42g) to the Caspian Tern (670g).

Globally, 11 species regularly breed inland, on islands or sandbanks along large rivers or in shallow wetlands. Some move to coastal waters when not breeding, but others remain at inland wetlands year-round. Most other species are coastal breeders and foragers, regularly returning to land to roost. However, the *Onychoprion* terns and noddies are truly pelagic. Sooty Terns are among the most aerial of birds, with immatures spending several years on the wing.

Like gannets and boobies, most terns feed by plunge diving, using their momentum to carry them to their prey. However, their smaller size and less streamlined shape on entering the water means that they seldom dive >1m. Their foraging aggregations often indicate the presence of predatory fish pushing small fish to the surface, and are used by fishers to locate fish schools. Terns also capture prey by surface seizing, or snatching prey out of the air. Some species take insects, frogs and other animals from vegetation, and some even feed on foot.

The sexes look alike, but males average slightly larger than females. Most species undergo a complete post-breeding moult and a partial pre-breeding moult, resulting in distinct non-breeding and breeding plumages. Some species replace their inner primaries twice, resulting in strong contrast between silvery-grey fresh inner primaries and older, blackish outer primaries. A few species have erratic primary moult, with multiple active moult centres. Juvenile body plumage is replaced within a few months of fledging.

Terns are typically monogamous and retain the same mate in successive years. Pairs undertake aerial displays, and courtship feeding plays a large

Ad Greater Crested (Swift) Tern coming in to land

role in pair bond formation and maintenance. Most are colonial breeders, mobbing intruders, shrieking at and even striking them. Terns nest in a wide range of habitats, from islands and cliffs to beaches, gravel plains and wetlands. They lay 1–3 well-camouflaged eggs. A replacement clutch is often laid if the first clutch is lost. Both sexes incubate and feed the semi-precocial chicks. Most species carry prey back to the nest in their bills, but some pelagic species regurgitate prey. The chicks are fed for several weeks after fledging, dispersing from the colony with their parents and continuing to beg noisily for food.

Most terns are gregarious, foraging, travelling and roosting in flocks. They also are migratory, or at least nomadic, moving to exploit seasonally abundant food resources. Long-distance migrants typically break their migration at a series of staging areas, where they spend a few weeks accumulating fat reserves before resuming their migrations.

Only 7 of the 47 species are globally threatened and 4 are Near Threatened. Proportionally, the tiny *Sternula* terns, which breed singly or in loose colonies along the coast, are most at risk. The southern African representative of this genus, the Damara Tern, is Near Threatened globally, but is Critically Endangered in South Africa, where fewer than 50 pairs survive.

Greater Crested Terns in full breeding plumage at the start of the breeding season

Caspian Tern *Hydroprogne caspia*

47–54cm; 580–750g

The largest tern. Very heavy red or orange-red bill with a black tip is diagnostic. In flight, dark primaries form a large blackish tip to the underwing. Cap is black in br plumage, variably streaked white in non-br plumage. Larger and darker above than West African Crested Tern (p.170), with heavier, redder bill and less deeply forked tail. Juv has brown fringes to back and scapulars, darker grey tail and flight feathers, and a dull orange bill. **Voice:** Deep, harsh *'kraaak'*; recently fledged chicks have a whining, begging call. **Status and biology:** Some 70,000 pairs breed in N America, Eurasia, Africa, Australia and New Zealand. Not threatened globally, but **VULNERABLE** in Namibia and South Africa, where the total breeding population is some 600 pairs, mainly in South Africa; small numbers breed in Namibia, Botswana and on Europa Island, Mozambique Channel. Locally common resident at large wetlands and coastal waters; often feeds over the surf zone, especially where diatom blooms attract mullets. Usually breeds in small colonies, often in association with gulls and other waterbirds. Breeds mainly in winter at Lake St Lucia, but in summer elsewhere in the region; lays 2 (1–3) eggs in a shallow scrape. Eats a wide diversity of fish, especially mullet and gobies. Reusesterretjie

Br ad with a full black cap early in the breeding season

Non-br ad showing grizzled cap

Br ad showing dark underwing tips

Recently fledged juv showing mottled scapulars and orange bill

West African Crested Tern *Thalasseus albididorsalis* 46–48cm; 340–420g

A large, pale tern with a yellow-orange bill; recently split from the New World Royal Tern. Smaller than Caspian Tern (p.169), with a more slender, relatively longer bill that lacks a dark tip; in flight, primaries are greyish (not black) on underwing. Most likely to be confused with Greater Crested Tern (p.172), but bill more orange; outer primaries darker grey, contrasting with paler coverts and back. Appreciably larger than Lesser Crested (p.173) and Elegant terns, with a heavier bill. Br ads have full black crown with shaggy crest. Non-br ads have extensive white forehead and crown, with often only a small black nuchal patch. Juv has mottled brown wing coverts. Imm has dark carpal bar. **Voice:** Loud, harsh '*ree-ack*'. **Status and biology:** Breeds along the W coast of Africa from Mauritania to Guinea; winters N to Morocco and S to N Namibia. Fairly common south to Ilha dos Tigres, sthn Angola, and may be regular at the Cunene River mouth in summer; vagrant S to Walvis Bay. Eats fish and crustaceans; often crabs. Koningsterretjie

Flock of non-br ads in central Angola

Br ad with black cap extending to bill (cf. Greater Crested Tern, p.172)

Non-br ad; note grey wing tips

Non-br ad in moult

Br ad showing dark grey outer primaries

Elegant Tern *Thalasseus elegans*

38–41cm; 200–320g

Slightly larger than Lesser Crested (p.173) and Sandwich (p.174) terns; orange bill longer and more slender than in Lesser Crested, with a drooped tip; underwing tips dark grey. Paler grey above than Lesser Crested Tern, with a whitish (not pale grey) rump that contrasts with the darker grey back, and a longer, shaggier crest. Appreciably smaller than West African Crested Tern, with a longer, more slender bill. Br ad has full black cap. Non-br ad has black hind crown (more extensive than in West African Crested Tern, extending in front of eye). First-winter birds have dark carpal bar and some dark-centred wing coverts; bill less richly orange, but more so than in juv Lesser Crested Tern. **Voice:** Grating call similar to that of Sandwich Tern. **Status and biology: NEAR THREATENED.** Some 15,000–25,000 pairs breed from S California to N Mexico; migrate south along the west coast of S America to central Chile. Vagrant; birds apparently of this species recorded several times in the W Cape and Namibia, but identification complicated by hybrids with Sandwich Terns in France and Spain, as well as hybrids between Lesser Crested and Sandwich terns. Also hybridises with Cabot's Terns (the American form of Sandwich Tern) at several sites on both the Pacific and Atlantic coasts of N America. Hybrids have shorter, more slender bills, often with some black marks. Eats mainly small fish. **Elegante Sterretjie**

Large flock in nthn Chile

Vagrant non-br ad with Greater Crested and Sandwich terns

Non-br ad Elegant Terns in Peru

Non-br ad showing pale upperparts and whitish rump

Non-br ad showing narrow blackish wing tips

Greater Crested (Swift) Tern *Thalasseus bergii* 46–49cm; 320–430g

A large tern with a long, slightly drooped yellow or greenish-yellow bill (not orange, as in West African Crested Tern (p.170), Lesser Crested and Elegant (p.171) terns). Appreciably larger than Lesser Crested and Elegant terns. Br ads have a black cap and shaggy crest, but have a small white frons (black extends to bill in other crested terns). Non-br ads have a white forecrown. Back pale grey in nominate race; darker grey in *T. b. velox* from the tropical Indian Ocean, which may reach Mozambique. Juv has a shorter, dull yellow bill; upperparts mottled blackish-brown with blackish margins to flight feathers, appearing dark grey in flight. Imm retains dark flight feathers. Legs usually black, but some juvs have yellow-orange legs. **Voice:** Harsh '*kree-eck*'; juv has a thin, whistled begging call. **Status and biology:** At least 50,000 pairs breed from Namibia through the tropical Indian Ocean to Australia and islands in the south-central Pacific Ocean. Nominate race is endemic to sthn Africa; 8,000–15,000 pairs breed at islands and coastal wetlands from central Namibia to Algoa Bay; numbers increasing. Common resident and local migrant in coastal waters, up to 20km offshore; also estuaries and coastal wetlands. Breeds in large colonies, sometimes in association with gulls. Lays 1 egg (rarely 2) in a shallow scrape. Eats mainly pelagic fish, especially anchovy (South Africa) and pelagic gobies (Namibia); also occasional squid, crustaceans and crickets. Takes some insects in flight, often soaring high over land. Large numbers follow the sardine run along the east coast in winter, but juvs from the W Cape also disperse north to central Namibia. Geelbeksterretjie

Juv showing dark, scaly upperwing and diffuse cap

Br ad showing white frons

Non-br ad showing grizzled forecrown; juv moulting into first winter plumage (inset)

Lesser Crested Tern *Thalasseus bengalensis*

35–37cm; 180–240g

A medium-sized tern, slightly smaller than Sandwich Tern (p.174), with a fairly stout, orange-yellow bill. Smaller, more graceful and generally paler above than Greater Crested Tern; bill lacks drooped tip. Much smaller than West African Crested Tern (p.170); bill more slender. Main identification risk is vagrant Elegant Tern (p.171). Juv has mottled blackish-brown back and wing coverts, and dark grey flight feathers. First-winter birds retain dark grey flight feathers, darker carpal bar and some dark-centred wing coverts. **Voice:** Hoarse '*kreck*'. **Status and biology:** At least 60,000 pairs breed locally along the N African coast, through the Red and Arabian seas and N Indian Ocean, to Indonesia and N Australia. Locally fairly common non-br visitor to the tropical east coast, mainly in summer. Up to 3,000 birds occur along the Mozambique coast and in nthn KZN, probably originating from large colonies in the Red Sea. Vagrant farther south and west, where caution is needed with possible hybrids with Sandwich Terns as well as Elegant x Sandwich hybrids. One hybrid Sandwich Tern x Lesser Crested Tern from a colony in Mauritania was observed in the E Cape in Mar 2005. Most birds are present Oct–Apr; a few overwinter in the region. Forages in inshore waters, bays and estuaries; roosts along coast and at wetlands. Eats mainly small fish. **Kuifkopsterretjie**

Non-br ad

Non-br ad showing pale underwing tip

Non-br ad showing uniform upperparts with pale grey rump

First winter (left) has a duller, more yellow bill than non-br ads (centre and right)

173

Sandwich Tern *Thalasseus sandvicensis* 36–40cm; 190–240g

A very pale, medium-sized tern. Bill black with a yellow tip and longer and more slender than in Gull-billed Tern. In flight, has white (not grey) rump and more strongly forked tail. Br ad has black cap, and breast has faint pinkish wash in fresh plumage. Non-br ads have white forecrown, often with black mottling confined to nuchal collar. Juv is mottled above with darker flight feathers, but body coverts mostly replaced by the time they arrive in sthn Africa; bill tip dark, turning yellow by Dec. Imm has some dark outer primaries remaining from juv plumage. **Voice:** Loud '*kirik*'; often noisy prior to migrating north in autumn. **Status and biology:** Some 80,000–130,000 pairs breed in Europe and W Asia; recently split from the American form, Cabot's Tern *T. acuflavidus*. Occasionally hybridises with Lesser Crested and Elegant terns in Europe; hybrids tend to have yellow bills and can be confused with Lesser Crested and Elegant terns. A common migrant to coastal waters, estuaries and bays in sthn Africa; at least 20,000 birds originate mainly from W European breeding grounds. Numbers peak Oct–Apr, but some remain year-round. One pair bred in a colony of Greater Crested Terns and Hartlaub's Gulls on Halifax Island, Lüderitz, in May 2014, and has twice been suspected of breeding in tern colonies on W Cape islands. Eats mainly small fish. Grootsterretjie

Br ad with full black cap

Non-br ad showing little black in wing tip

First winter showing blackish outer primaries (top) and juv (above)

Gull-billed Tern *Gelochelidon nilotica*

35–38cm; 180–300g

A very pale, relatively long-legged tern with a rather stubby black bill. Similar in size to Sandwich Tern, but is heavier-bodied and broader-winged, with shorter, shallow-forked tail and shorter, more robust black bill that lacks a yellow tip; rump and tail grey (not white). Br ad has a full black cap. Non-br birds have mostly white crown with a black smudge behind eye; could be confused with non-br Whiskered Terns (p.193), but are appreciably larger and heavier-billed. Juv is mottled brown above; legs greyish (black in ad). **Voice:** Deep '*kaak*' and '*kek-kek*'. **Status and biology:** Some 30,000–50,000 pairs breed locally in California–Mexico, Ecuador–Peru, E USA–Argentina and across Eurasia. The Australasian race *G. n. macrotarsa* is sometimes split as a separate species. Rare vagrant to coastal lagoons and wetlands throughout the region, but most records are from the north and east. Records scattered year-round. Sometimes forages over fields and reedbeds near water. Eats fish, frogs, crabs and other invertebrates. Oostelike Sterretjie

Non-br ad searching for prey

Non-br ad showing fairly extensive black wing tip

Non-br ad with mostly white crown

Br ad with full black cap and pale grey upperparts

175

Black-naped Tern *Sterna sumatrana* 30cm; 95–120g

A small, very pale tern that is unusual in moulting only once a year. Ad has a neat black band extending from the lores through the eye, and broadening across nape; crown pure white; superficially resembles a tiny non-br Sandwich Tern (p.174), but bill entirely black. In flight, only outer web of outer primary is black. Underparts sometimes suffused pink. Juv has crown feathers tipped with black, and is mottled brown above; moults directly into ad plumage, but moult protracted; older imms resemble ads but with a dusky carpal bar and a variable black patch on the ear coverts. **Voice:** Clipped, repeated *'ki-ki'*. **Status and biology:** Population poorly known; breeds at tropical islands across the N Indian Ocean through SE Asia and N Australia to the central Pacific Ocean. Rare vagrant to the east coast of sthn Africa from the tropical Indian Ocean; closest colonies are in the Seychelles, where the total population is <200 pairs. Disperses after breeding, regularly reaching the Comoros and Madagascar. All sthn African records Nov–Mar. Forages singly, usually close to land, but often roosts with other terns. Eats mainly small fish. Swartneksterretjie

Juv showing mottled, darker grey upperparts

Ad showing very pale plumage

A pair of adults; note the black outer web of the outer primary

Roseate Tern *Sterna dougallii*

33–38cm; 100–130g

A sleek, medium-sized tern with very pale grey upperparts and a long, slightly drooped, blackish bill. Legs and wings longer than in other medium-sized terns. Underwing appears all-white in flight. Br ads have full black cap, pink wash to breast, crimson legs, red bill base and long white outer tail feathers that project well beyond wings at rest. Non-br ads have white forecrown; best identified by long bill and pale colour. Juv finely barred blackish-brown above; differs from juv Antarctic Tern (p.180) by blacker cap, longer bill, greyer wings and more slender body. Imm retains some juv tertials and has darker upperwing coverts than non-br ad. **Voice:** Harsh '*chir-rik*' when breeding; also a grating '*aarh*'. **Status and biology:** Some 35,000 pairs breed locally along the coasts of eastern N America, W Europe and the tropical Indian Ocean south to Australia and South Africa. Not threatened globally, but **ENDANGERED** in South Africa given the very small breeding population; 140 pairs breed in winter (May–Oct) at small colonies on islands in Algoa Bay and on Dyer Island. Occurs among tern roosts sporadically in W and E Cape; most reliably at Cape Recife, Gqeberha, where it bred in the 1960s. Lays 1 or 2 eggs in a shallow scrape. Non-br vagrants may occur along the Mozambique coast from populations breeding in the tropical Indian Ocean (closest colonies in W Madagascar). Eats small fish. Rooiborssterretjie

Br ads in display flight, showing pale upperparts and long tail streamers; br ad from below (inset)

Br ads showing variable colour of long, drooped bills; first winter, with faint dark carpal bar (inset)

Common Tern *Sterna hirundo*

31–35cm; 100–160g

Typically the commonest medium-sized tern; often found in large flocks. Differs from Arctic Tern by its longer bill and legs, and greyish (not white) rump and tail. Primaries have broader black webs than in Arctic and Antarctic (p.180) terns, visible in flight as darker panel on upper- and underwing. Less dumpy than Antarctic Tern, with a more slender bill; ads usually lack grey wash on underparts and bill and legs seldom bright red. Bill shorter and less drooped than in Roseate Tern (p.177); upperparts darker grey. Best told from vagrant White-cheeked Tern (p.182) by its pale grey rump and tail that contrast with the darker grey back (not uniform grey) and different underwing pattern (see that species). In br plumage, has black-tipped red bill (rarely all red), light grey wash to breast, and short tail streamers (level with folded wing tips) relative to those of Arctic Tern. Juv mottled brown above but moults before reaching sthn Africa. Imm has conspicuous dark carpal bars. **Voice:** '*Kik-kik*' and '*kee-arh*'. **Status and biology:** At least 500,000 pairs breed across E and central N America and Eurasia, with outlying populations in the Caribbean, Senegal, Nigeria and Cameroon. Winters farther south, with many individuals migrating across the equator. A once-abundant migrant to coastal waters and adjacent wetlands in sthn Africa, its numbers have decreased in recent years. However, more than 100,000 birds still visit the region, mainly from breeding grounds around the Baltic Sea. Numbers peak Oct–Apr, but some imms remain year-round. Eats small fish and crustaceans. Gewone Sterretjie

Pre-br ad often has grey-washed underparts

Imm showing prominent dark carpal bar

Post-br ad losing its full black cap; note longish legs

Imm showing dull red base to its bill

Arctic Tern *Sterna paradisaea*

33–35cm; 90–130g

Similar to Common Tern, but more elegant and compact, with a shorter neck, shorter, finer bill and paler outer primaries in flight; rump and tail white (not pale grey). At rest, legs distinctly shorter. Not as dumpy as Antarctic Tern (p.180), especially at rest; bill smaller; bill and legs usually blackish (not red). Br ad has full black cap, pale grey wash on breast, dark red bill and legs; tail streamers extend beyond folded wing (but growing feathers are shorter). Non-br ad has extensive white frons, and blackish bill and legs. Imm has a darker carpal bar, but not as strongly developed as in imm Common Tern. **Voice:** '*Kik-kik*' given in flight. **Status and biology:** Around 1 million pairs breed throughout the N Holarctic zone and migrate south to the Southern Ocean each year in the longest animal migration. Fairly common migrant to coastal and oceanic waters off sthn Africa; ringing recoveries suggest that most birds come from W Europe. Most migrate through oceanic waters; seldom roost ashore. Birds from Greenland and Iceland spend 10–15 weeks travelling off the African or S American coasts on their southbound migration (Sept–Oct), spend 5 months mainly in the Weddell Sea, then return more rapidly (5–7 weeks in Apr–May) to their colonies along a more direct route through the mid-Atlantic Ocean (see map p.12). Usually seen in small flocks at sea; sometimes roost on the water. Eats small fish and crustaceans. Arktiese Sterretjie

Non-br ad; note white rump

First winter imm showing faint dark carpal bar and short legs

Br ad with red bill, greyish breast and long tail streamers

Juv showing translucent flight feathers

Antarctic Tern *Sterna vittata*

34–40cm; 110–170g

A rather dumpy, medium-sized tern, with a heavier bill than either Arctic (p.179) or Common (p.178) terns. Leg length varies among races from short to fairly long. Br ad has a full black cap, bright red bill and legs, and grey underparts contrasting with a white cheek stripe. Told from vagrant White-cheeked Tern (p.182) by its white (not grey) rump and full red bill. Non-br ad has paler grey underparts and a white forecrown, but retains red legs and some red in bill (black in non-br Common and Arctic terns). Imm has black bill and legs; best told apart by heavy bill and dumpy body; some retain a few barred juv tertials. Juv has chequered brown, grey and white upperparts and diffuse brown wash on sides of breast; differs from juv Roseate Tern (p.177) by its shorter, heavier bill and paler cap.

Voice: High-pitched '*kik-kik*' and harsher '*kreaah*'. **Status and biology:** Not threatened globally, but **ENDANGERED** in South Africa given the very small breeding population at the Prince Edward Islands. Some 40,000–50,000 pairs breed at sub-Antarctic islands and the Antarctic Peninsula in summer; 850 pairs at Tristan da Cunha and Gough Island, and 10–20 pairs at the Prince Edward Islands. Fairly common winter migrant to coastal waters in sthn Africa, mostly Apr–Oct. Breeds singly or in small colonies, often on cliffs; lays 1 or 2 eggs. Eats small fish and crustaceans. At some breeding islands it also eats terrestrial invertebrates, occasionally foraging on foot. **Grysborssterretjie**

Non-br ad

Non-br ad showing red bill and white rump

First winter

Br ad with full black cap

Recently fledged juv

Kerguelen Tern *Sterna virgata*

32–34cm; 90–150g

Localised endemic confined to sub-Antarctic islands in the SW Indian Ocean. A darker version of Antarctic Tern with the petite structure of an Arctic Tern (p.179). Ad has more strongly contrasting white cheek stripe and grey wash on rump and outer tail; tail streamers shorter than in Antarctic Tern. Br ad has full black cap and red bill and legs; non-br ad has white frons and blackish bill and legs. Juv sooty grey-brown above, finely spotted whitish; breast mottled grey-brown, darker than juv Antarctic Tern. Imm similar to non-br ad, but retains some juv wing coverts. **Voice:** High-pitched *'kik-kik'*. **Status and biology:** NEAR THREATENED globally, but ENDANGERED in South Africa given the very small breeding population at Prince Edward Islands. Population less than 2,000 pairs: 55 pairs at Prince Edward islands, 200 pairs at Crozets and 1,500 pairs at Kerguelen islands. Breeds in summer, singly or in small, loose colonies, often some distance from the sea. Lays 1 or 2 eggs in a shallow scrape next to a sheltering rock or low plant. Eats fish, crustaceans and terrestrial invertebrates; more often forages over coastal mires than do Antarctic Terns. Kerguelense Sterretjie

Br ad starting to lose black frons

Br ad showing dark grey underparts and short tail streamers

First winter

Juv moulting into first winter plumage

Recently fledged juv

White-cheeked Tern *Sterna repressa*

32–35cm; 80–105g

A medium-sized tern, resembling a dark Common Tern (p.178); differs from this (and Arctic (p.179) and Antarctic (p.180) terns) in having a uniform grey back, rump and tail. In flight, underwing shows a diffuse pale centre, contrasting with grey lesser coverts and darker grey flight feathers. Br ads have grey underparts, darkest on belly; could be confused with br plumage of Whiskered Tern (p.193), but is larger, with a longer bill, forked tail and dusky grey (not white) vent. Imm white below with mostly black cap and dark carpal bar; best told from imm Common Tern by grey rump and tail, darker grey upperwings and broad, dark grey trailing edge to underwing. **Voice:** Ringing

'kee-leck'. **Status and biology:** Some 100,000–200,000 pairs breed from N Kenya through the Red Sea and Arabian Peninsula locally to W India. Rare vagrant to the east coast; most records have been in roosts of other terns during summer. Often feeds well offshore when not breeding, foraging in large flocks with other pelagic seabirds over schools of tuna or dolphins. Eats small fish and invertebrates. **Witwangsterretjie**

Flock of non-br ads and imms

Br ad at its colony

First winter showing heavy bill and blackish underwing tips

Br ad and chick

Damara Tern *Sternula balaenarum*

21–23cm; 46–60g

A very small, rather uniform pale grey tern with narrow wings and rapid wing beats. Differs from Little (p.184) and Saunders's (p.185) terns in having a longer, slightly droop-tipped bill and more uniform upperwing; body appears shorter and more dumpy in flight. Br ad has diagnostic full black cap and bill. Non-br ads and imms have pale crown, more similar to Saunders's Tern than Little Tern, but usually grizzled grey (not white). Juv has buffy-brown barring on mantle, and horn-coloured bill base. **Voice:** Far-carrying, rapid '*chit-ick*', higher-pitched than Little Tern. **Status and biology:** Near-endemic; breeds from S Angola to Algoa Bay. Not threatened globally but **NEAR THREATENED** in Namibia (up to 2,500 pairs) and **CRITICALLY ENDANGERED** in South Africa, where <50 pairs survive, mostly in Algoa Bay. Favours sheltered coastlines, bays and lagoons. Breeds on coastal dunes and saltpans in summer, singly or in loose colonies up to 10km inland. Lays a single egg; many chicks follow ads to sea as soon as they can flutter. Most migrate to W Africa in winter, but some remain year-round. Eats mainly small fish. Damarasterretjie

Br ad showing uniform grey back and rump

Non-br ad showing darker outer primaries

Juv showing brownish wing coverts

Non-br ad; pale crown extends farther back than in Little Tern

Br ad with full black cap, at its nest site

Little Tern *Sternula albifrons*

22–24cm; 45–60g

A tiny tern, most likely to be confused with rare Saunders's Tern. Similar in size to Damara Tern (p.183), but bill is shorter and straighter; typically has greater contrast between dark outer primaries (but less marked than Saunders's Tern) and rest of upperwing. Br ad has orange-red legs, a yellow bill with a small black tip, and white forehead extends above eye (confined to frons in Saunders's Tern); rump and tail paler grey than back. However, seldom seen in full br plumage in region. Non-br ads have white crown streaked dark grey, giving a hint of a white eyebrow; bill mostly black; back, rump and central tail uniform grey. Juv mottled grey-brown above with fairly uniform upperwing. **Voice:** Slightly rasping '*ket-ket*'. **Status and biology:** Some 70,000–100,000 pairs breed at coastal and inland sites throughout Eurasia and W Africa through SE Asia to Australia. Non-br migrant to coastal waters, estuaries and adjacent wetlands down the east coast; common locally in Mozambique, becoming increasingly scarce to the W Cape; rare north of the Berg River estuary (mainly at the Orange River mouth and Sandwich Harbour). Most occur Oct–Apr, but a few overwinter in the northeast. Sthn African birds probably from E European or central Asian populations given their apparent migration down the E African coast. Mainly feeds close inshore on small fish and invertebrates. Kleinsterretjie

Br ad; white frons extends to above eye

Non-br ad

Non-br ad showing white eyebrow and more uniform grey upperparts

Non-br ad with unusually pale hind crown

Br ad has narrow white trailing edge to secondaries

Saunders's Tern *Sternula saundersi*

22–24cm; 45–60g

Very similar to Little Tern, but paler with greater contrast to blackish outer primaries and broader white trailing edge to secondaries; bill averages slightly shorter and heavier. Br ad has 'square' white forehead confined to frons (extends above eye in Little Tern); legs dull red-brown; bill richer yellow; lacks a blackish line at the base of the bill. Non-br ads are paler above than Little Tern with more extensive white crown (no hint of white eyebrow); blackish carpal bar contrasts strongly with paler hindwing. Juv lightly mottled brown above, paler and more ginger on crown than juv Little Tern; wing pattern much more contrasting, recalling Sabine's Gull. Juv and imm show indistinct darker carpal bars. **Voice:** *'Kwit'* call reported to be less rasping than Little Tern's. **Status and biology:** Population is poorly known, with only a few colonies studied, but probably several thousand pairs breed at coastal sites from Somalia to India, Sri Lanka and the Maldives; non-breeding birds disperse south along the east African coast. Rare non-br migrant to coastal Mozambique; to date, only confirmed from San Sebastian Peninsula and the Bazaruto Archipelago, where a few occur year-round. Adults in br plumage recorded in all months except Mar–Apr; courtship feeding observed in Sep. Feeds up to 15km offshore mainly on small fish, crustaceans and other invertebrates. **Arabiese Sterretjie**

Br ad; square white frons just reaches eyes

Non-br ad showing whitish crown and pale grey upperparts contrasting with blackish outer primaries

Br ad has broad white trailing edge to secondaries

Non-br ad wing from below

Moulting ad and first winter

Sooty Tern *Onychoprion fuscatus*

40–44cm; 150–240g

A fairly large, long-winged, dark-backed tern. Larger and darker above than Bridled Tern, with broader white frons that does not extend behind eye; black crown does not contrast with back. In flight, both species have bold white leading edge to upperwing. Juvs and imms have blackish throat and breast (Bridled Terns are white below); could potentially be confused with noddies or imm jaegers, but has whitish belly and underwing coverts. **Voice:** Loud '*wick-a-wick*' or '*wide-awake*' uttered at colonies, when feeding in flocks at sea or when attracted to ships' lights at night. Alarm is harsh '*kraark*'. **Status and biology:** The most abundant tern with >10 million pairs breeding at tropical islands worldwide; some 5 million pairs breed in the W Indian Ocean, including 760,000 pairs at Europa Island, Mozambique Channel. Common non-breeding visitor to oceanic waters off Mozambique and nthn KZN. Typically remains well offshore, but large numbers may be wrecked ashore or blown inland by tropical cyclones. Lays a single egg in a shallow scrape on the ground, or directly onto rock. Seldom rests on water; remains aloft at night. Juvs remain at sea for 4–5 years before returning to breeding islands, apparently flying continuously. Eats squid, fish and invertebrates; picks prey from surface, often feeding in association with predatory fish and dolphins, and at night. **Roetsterretjie**

Ad's white frons just reaches the eye

Juv has mostly brown underparts with white belly and off-white underwing coverts

Ad shows little contrast between blackish cap and dark brown back

Ad's dark flight feathers contrast with white belly and underwing coverts

Bridled Tern *Onychoprion anaethetus*

30–32cm; 90–160g

An elegant, dark-backed tern. Smaller than Sooty Tern, with paler, brown-grey upperparts. Narrow white frons extends behind eye, and dark crown contrasts with paler back. Non-br ads have white spotting on crown. Juvs and imms have wing coverts finely edged buffy white, and white underparts (not blackish as in juv Sooty Tern). **Voice:** '*Wup-wup*' and '*kee-arr*'.

Status and biology: Global population poorly known; several hundred thousand pairs breed at tropical islands worldwide, with 140,000 pairs in the Red Sea alone; smaller colonies on the Somali coast and the Seychelles. Rare non-br visitor to oceanic waters off Mozambique from tropical Indian Ocean colonies; vagrant elsewhere. One bird returned repeatedly to the tern roost at Cape Recife for several years. Eats small fish, squid and invertebrates. Brilsterretjie

Ad showing long white supercilium

Ad in flight appears slightly smaller than Sooty Tern

Ad showing dark cap contrasting with paler back

Ad's flight feathers have paler bases than ad Sooty Tern

Ad upperparts can become quite faded when worn; juv showing pale-tipped back and wing feathers (inset)

187

NODDIES AND WHITE TERN

Noddies are dark brown or grey tropical terns. Flight loose and buoyant; tail long and wedge-shaped in the brown species found in our region, with a shallow central notch when fanned. Seldom visit land away from breeding colonies.

The brown noddies could be confused with immature Sooty Tern (p.186), but lack whitish underwing coverts and pale belly. The White (or Fairy) Tern is an all-white tropical tern most closely related to the noddies.

White Tern *Gygis alba*

23–30cm; 90–155g

A fairly small, all-white tern with a strangely rounded head, a distinctive up-tilted bill, and black eyes accentuated by blackish feathers around them. At close range, blackish shafts to outer primaries are visible. Fresh plumage juv has buff barring mainly on upperparts, but this is soon lost, and unlikely to be seen in vagrants reaching sthn Africa. **Voice:** Rasping '*krieek krieek*', seldom heard away from colonies. **Status and biology:** Global population poorly known; perhaps 100,000 pairs breed at tropical islands worldwide. Taxonomy debated, with up to 3 species recognised. Nominate subspecies from the Atlantic Ocean has more slender bill with a less extensive blue base than Indo-Pacific *G. a. candida*. Closest colonies to the region are on St Helena, the Seychelles and Mascarene Islands. Vagrant to sthn Africa; only one record from Kei River Mouth in Dec 2018, presumably from western Indian Ocean population. Breeds singly or in loose colonies; famously lays a single egg on a tree branch, with no vestige of a nest. Eats small fish, squid and crustaceans. **Feesterretjie**

Ad growing outer tail feathers

Wings often appear translucent

Striking white plumage is diagnostic

Up-tilted bill has bluish base

Brown Noddy *Anous stolidus*

36–44cm; 150–220g

Larger and browner than Lesser Noddy (p.190), with a shorter, heavier bill; pale crown contrasts sharply with blackish-brown lores. Shows greater contrast across wings due to paler brown greater upperwing coverts and central underwing. Juv has pale crown reduced or absent. **Voice:** Hoarse '*kaark*', seldom heard away from colonies. **Status and biology:** Global population poorly known; several hundred thousand pairs breed at tropical islands worldwide; closest colonies in Indian Ocean are off N Madagascar. Some 600 pairs breed from Sept–Apr at Tristan da Cunha and Gough Island. Rare in oceanic waters off Mozambique; vagrant elsewhere, with most records in summer. Breeds singly or in loose colonies on the ground, on cliff ledges or in trees (at Tristan and Gough); lays a single egg. Eats small fish and squid. Grootbruinsterretjie

Ad showing heavy bill

Noddies have long, wedge-shaped tails

Secondaries are distinctly darker than coverts

Blackish lores are diagnostic

189

Lesser Noddy *Anous tenuirostris*

30–34cm; 90–125g

Smaller than Brown Noddy (p.189), with a longer, more slender bill. Whitish forehead merges with brown lores and ashy-grey crown extends further back onto nape, but these characters can be hard to see at sea, when both species tend to flee from approaching vessels. Upperwing and underwing are more uniformly dark brown than in Brown Noddy, but this varies with wear and moult in both species. Pale crown reduced or absent in juv. **Voice:** Short, rattling *'churrr'*; generally silent at sea. **Status and biology:** Breeds at tropical islands in the W Indian Ocean (250,000 pairs) and at islands off W Australia (50,000 pairs). Rare vagrant to sthn Africa, with all records Jan–May; nearest colonies are in the Seychelles and Mascarene Islands. Eats small fish and invertebrates. **Kleinbruinsterretjie**

Upperwing is more uniform than Brown Noddy's

Breeds in trees (Brown Noddies mostly on the ground)

Ad has long, slender bill and pale frons merging over the lores, appearing paler-headed than Brown Noddy

Often occur in small flocks at sea

Lesser Noddy (left) is slightly smaller and more slender than Brown Noddy (right)

LAKE TERNS

Small, mostly freshwater terns with square tails. Breeding plumages distinct, but non-br birds harder to separate. Often pick prey from the water surface rather than plunge-diving. 4 species globally, of which 3 occur in the region; 2 as non-br migrants from the northern hemisphere. Local species are not listed as Threatened, but numbers of White-winged Terns have decreased dramatically.

Black Tern *Chlidonias niger*

22–24cm; 55–75g

A dark-backed lake tern. In br plumage, black head, breast and belly merge into dark grey back and wings; lacks contrast of White-winged Tern (p.192). Non-br ad has diagnostic dark shoulder smudge, more extensive black on head than White-winged Tern, and no contrast between back, rump and tail. Darker than Whiskered Tern (p.193), with black cheek spot. Imm is slightly darker and less uniform above than non-br ad. **Voice:** Usually silent; flight call is quiet *'kik-kik'*. **Status and biology:** Some 250,000 pairs breed at wetlands in N America, Europe and W Asia, with the New World population likely to be split. Occasionally hybridises with White-winged Tern. Palearctic birds migrate mainly along the west coast of Africa; it is fairly common along the nthn Namibian coast from Dec–Apr, with stragglers reaching the W Cape. Smaller numbers travel down the Rift Valley, and might account for occasional records from the coast of KZN and inland wetlands. Occurs in open ocean, bays and coastal wetlands; usually forages at sea, but many roost ashore; vagrant inland. Eats mainly small crustaceans; also fishing wastes. Swartsterretjie

Br ad has pale underwings

Non-br ad from below

Non-br ad showing uniform grey back and rump

Non-br ad Black Tern

Non-br ad showing diagnostic black patch on side of breast

White-winged Tern *Chlidonias leucopterus* 20–22cm; 42–70g

The smallest lake tern, with a white rump in all plumages. Striking black-and-white in br plumage with pale grey upperwings and black underwing coverts; white rump and tail contrast with black back; legs bright red. Non-br ad is paler above than Black Tern (p.191), with black confined to rear of crown, and no black shoulder smudge. Imm has slight brown tips to upperpart feathers. **Voice:** Short *'kek-kek'*. **Status and biology:** Perhaps as many as 1 million pairs breed at wetlands from E Europe to China. Occasionally hybridises with Black Tern. Locally common migrant to sthn Africa from Oct–Apr; small numbers overwinter, especially in the north of the region, with large numbers on Lake Kariba. Its population has probably benefited from the creation of many perennial wetlands, and particularly sewage works and commercial saltpans, but its numbers have decreased dramatically at some locations over the last few decades. Found mainly at lakes, estuaries and marshes, but occasionally also in sheltered coastal bays. Eats small fish, insects and other invertebrates; takes some prey in the air.
Witvlerksterretjie

Ads moulting into breeding plumage

Non-br ad lacks black patch on side of breast and has a paler rump than Black Tern

Br ad has black underwing coverts

Non-br ad has more extensive white above eye than Black Tern; note short bill and long legs

Whiskered Tern *Chlidonias hybrida*

The largest lake tern with relatively long legs and a heavy bill. Dark grey underparts in br plumage diagnostic; superficially resembles White-cheeked Tern (p.182), but is smaller, with white (not dusky grey) vent and less deeply forked tail. Non-br birds are larger than other lake terns, lacking dark cheek patch extending below eye. Paler grey above than non-br Black Tern (p.191); rump pale grey (white in White-winged Tern). Juv is mottled brown on back. **Voice:** Repeated, hard '*zizz*'. **Status and biology:** Global population poorly known; at least 50,000 pairs breed locally at wetlands in Eurasia, Africa and Australia; fewer than 7,500 pairs estimated to breed in sthn Africa. Fairly common resident and intra-African migrant at wetlands and marshes; unlikely to occur at sea, but could be found in tern roosts at estuaries and coastal wetlands. Breeds in small colonies; lays 2 or 3 eggs on a mound of floating vegetation. Eats fish, frogs and aquatic invertebrates.

Witbaardsterretjie

Juv has grizzled crown and dusky mark on sides of breast

Non-br ad showing robust build and mainly white crown

Br ad showing dark grey underparts and whitish vent

Br ad showing uniform grey upperparts; transitional ad (inset)

In warm waters, flying fish outnumber seabirds and can even be confused with storm petrels

FLYING FISH AND SQUID

Seabirds are not the only flying beasts that birders encounter at sea. At water temperatures above around 20°C the oceans are replete with flying fish and flying squid – which is just as well, given the low densities of seabirds in these warmer waters. Birders can stay focused by observing these fascinating creatures as they are flushed by predators, or more usually, by the observer's ship. Trying to photograph them is even more challenging than capturing seabirds in flight, but can be equally rewarding. This section gives a brief introduction to the diversity of forms found off southern Africa, and hopefully will stimulate birders to gather more data on their diversity and distribution.

Why fly?

The tropics support a wide diversity of predatory fish, such as tunas, marlins, sailfish and dolphinfish, all of which feed on smaller pelagic fish or squid. This intense predation pressure favours the evolution of

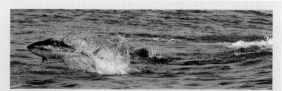

Flying fish 'fly' to escape gamefish such as tunas

strategies to reduce the risk of being eaten. However, there are few places to hide in the open ocean, and larger fish can swim faster than their prey. One of the few escapes is to jump out of the water. From below, the surface of the sea acts like a mirror, so anything leaping into the air effectively disappears until it re-enters the water. The halfbeaks can 'tail-walk' across the water surface to increase the distance between where they leave and re-enter, but flying fish take it to the next level. They also can change direction in flight, or land and then immediately take off again in a radically different direction to throw off any pursuing predator. Flight is not a new strategy to avoid being eaten; fossils of flying fish, unrelated to modern species, have been found dating back more than 200 million years.

FLYING FISH

Flying fish belong to the family Exocoetidae. They are closely related to the halfbeaks (Hemiramphidae), needlefish (Belonidae) and sauries (Scomberesocidae), which often leap out of the water to escape predators, but haven't evolved the enlarged fins needed to allow them to 'fly'. Flying fish use their specially modified pectoral and pelvic fins to glide low over the ocean surface to evade predatory fish and dolphins. When swimming, these fins lie flush against the body and the fish appears 'normal'. However, they are unusual in having an elongate lower tail fin, which allows them to prolong their flights.

Flying fish range in size from 2–50cm, with the largest weighing over 600g, but most are less than 30cm. As body size increases, wing length has to increase even faster, imposing an upper size limit because the folded pectoral fins cannot extend beyond the tail tip without significantly impeding swimming. In addition to their modified fins, they also have a stiffened spine and reinforced lower jaw which protects them from the impact of hitting the water at speeds of up to 60km/hour.

The 60–70 recognised species are placed in 7 genera. The main division is between the two-winged species (*Exocoetus* and *Fodiator*), which rely on the two pectoral fins for lift, and the four-winged species (*Cheilopogon, Cypselurus, Hirundichthys* and *Prognichthys*), which also use the pelvic fins for lift and flight control. The sailfin flying fish (*Parexocoetus*) have intermediate-sized pelvic fins and an enlarged dorsal fin, which can be tilted over to generate additional lift. Four-winged species have longer, narrower pectoral fins than two-winged species, giving them a better lift-to-drag ratio and allowing them to glide for longer. Four-winged species were the inspiration for the biplane design that featured prominently in the early development of aircraft. It is not always easy to see the pelvic fins, which are closed at times during a flight. The most obviously four-winged specimens are the tiny juvenile flying fish or 'smurfs', which can have the pelvic fins almost as well developed as the pectoral fins. They resemble dragonflies, and make short, often erratic, looping flights, which makes them almost impossible to photograph.

A Red-footed Booby catches a large flying fish in the air

The threat from behind

Escaping predators from below is all very well, but it exposes flying fish to predation risk in the air. Several seabirds, especially boobies and frigatebirds, catch flying fish in the air. Boobies have learned to accompany ships to target the flying fish they flush. Red-footed Boobies, the smallest and most agile booby species, are particularly adept at this. On windy days they cruise effortlessly in the updraft created by the ship, whereas on calm days they perch on the foremast, waiting for a fish to take to the air. The flying fish are not entirely defenceless – they can change their wing angle to dive into the water if threatened, but they seem to struggle to detect boobies approaching directly from behind, and are often caught.

Unfortunately, relating what is seen at sea to this traditional taxonomy is complicated by post-mortem changes in colour and even apparent fin shape. Birders in the Pacific and N Atlantic have photographed more than 50 varieties, but have struggled to link them to described species. Instead they have devised an informal set of names for the various types. I have followed this system to suggest common names for some of the more distinctive forms found off sthn Africa, where the diversity of forms is even less well known. There appear to be only a few species around much of the coast of South Africa, but diversity increases considerably off KwaZulu-Natal and Mozambique.

The smaller forms and two-winged species often flush in schools of 10–50 fish, whereas the larger four-winged species typically flush singly or in smaller groups of 2–10 individuals, which may contain multiple species. Flying fish feed mainly on zooplankton and are often the most abundant small pelagic fish in tropical oceans. They lay buoyant eggs at the sea surface or attach their eggs to floating debris (which has been suggested as a reason for the frequent ingestion of plastic by N Pacific albatrosses). The larval fish hatch within a few weeks, and grow quickly, apparently maturing within 1–2 years. The larger species are the target of commercial fisheries, but no species is listed as Threatened.

Do they really fly?

If flight is defined as propulsion through the air, flying fish and squid should really be called gliding fish and squid, because they obtain all their momentum from the water. Flying fish use a quick snap of the body to lift them out of the water and into the glide. In larger individuals, this is accompanied by a series of rapid tail flicks, which further accelerates them and allows them to glide for considerable distances. Flying squid are jet propelled, driven by squirting water forcefully from their mouths. Both groups benefit from the ground effect, which increases the lift generated by travelling low over the

Flying fish can extend flights by beating the lower tail fin in the water to gain extra speed and lift

water surface. Flight speeds are not well documented, but are suggested to be around 60km/hour. Flying fish can undertake impressive flights thanks to their ability to accelerate again by beating their lower tail fin in the water, leaving a sinuous track across the water surface. Long flights, lasting over 30 seconds and covering up to 500m, typically involve a series of 5–8 such 'boosts'. Accelerating in flight is easy in calm conditions, but can lead to mishaps in choppy seas if they fail to engage with a wave trough, or crash into a wave crest.

Most glides end when the fish hits the water, but sometimes they elect to dive by changing their wing angle

Dazzling diversity

At first glance, flying fish look fairly similar, but digital photographs reveal a stunning array of colours and wing patterns. This page shows taxa photographed off southern Africa.

Large Clearwing

Small Clearwing

Delta Cenizo

Fenestrated Naffwing

Purple Bandwing

Indian Midnightwing

Yellow Bandwing

Blue Bandwing

Mozambique Cerulean

Spotted Pinkwing

Thrushwing

Tawny Leopardwing

Red-spot Midget

Oddspot Midget (Sailfin Flying Fish)

FLYING SQUID

Flying squid are even less well known than flying fish. Flying squid apparently all belong to one family, the Ommastrephidae, which have over 20 species in 11 genera, but it is unknown how many species 'fly'. It seems that it is only the smaller, perhaps immature individuals that fly, but even this is not well established. At sea off southern Africa, these animals range from around 10–30 cm in flight. They usually flush in groups of 10–80 animals, but occasionally only one or two will take flight at once, and occasionally they even join small groups of flying fish.

Flying squid are jet propelled, using water ejected from their mouths to propel them into the air. They are unique among flying animals in travelling backwards. On a calm day you can hear a group 'spisss' as they emerge from the water, each trailing a jet of water. They also are the only animals that have wings at the front and back of the body, rather than on either side. The leading wing is formed by the fins on the side of the mantle, which are expanded somewhat compared to non-flying squid. But the trailing wing is more bizarre – formed from the tentacles, which have lateral flaps of translucent skin to increase their surface area. Quite how they join to form a coherent wing, and what consequences these modifications to the tentacles might have on their more traditional function underwater, have not been studied.

Unlike flying fish, flying squid cannot prolong their glide because they must land in the water to 'reload' their propulsion system. They usually glide at most 10–20m, which makes them a lot more challenging to photograph. There appear to be

Flying squid have green photophores above the eyes

two forms around sthn Africa. The most common and widespread form has a blue-grey body with fine greenish spots. It is most common in the warm waters off the east coast, but also occurs in the Agulhas Current south of Africa, and locally in oceanic waters of the S Atlantic. A reddish form in the Mozambique Channel usually occurs in separate groups, but mixed groups have been seen. Whether it is a different species is unknown.

Flying squid usually take off in groups; most appear greyish, but a reddish form (centre) occurs in the Mozambique Channel

INDEX

Index